IT ALL STARTED
WITH COLUMBUS

FERDINAND AND ISABELLA REFUSED TO BELIEVE THE WORLD
WAS ROUND, EVEN WHEN COLUMBUS SHOWED THEM AN EGG.

It all started with Columbus

BEING AN UNEXPURGATED, UNABRIDGED, AND UNLIKELY HISTORY OF THE UNITED STATES FROM CHRISTOPHER COLUMBUS TO RICHARD M. NIXON FOR THOSE WHO, HAVING PERUSED A VOLUME OF HISTORY IN SCHOOL, SWORE THEY WOULD NEVER READ ANOTHER.

BY RICHARD ARMOUR, A.B., C.D., E.F.

Lavishly illustrated by CAMPBELL GRANT

McGraw-Hill Book Company

New York • St. Louis • San Francisco • Düsseldorf
Mexico • Montreal • Panama • Rio de Janeiro • Toronto

Library of Congress Catalog Card Number: 61–17597

First McGraw-Hill Paperback Edition, 1971

456789 MUMU 79876

07-002298-4

PRINTED IN THE UNITED STATES OF AMERICA

HUMBLY

DEDICATED

IN AN ATTITUDE OF GRATITUDE

TO **WALTER CARRUTHERS SELLAR**
AND **ROBERT JULIAN YEATMAN**
WHO WROTE THE WONDERFUL
1066 AND ALL THAT

ACKNOWLEDGMENT.

The author
wishes to thank
Christopher Columbus,
Captain John Smith, George
Washington, and the many others
who made this book possible. He is also
grateful to the Red Skins, the Red Coats, the
Red Badge of Courage, and the inventor of gun powder,
without whom the history of our country would
have been sadly lacking in bloodshed and
would have made dull reading.
Nota bene: The author will appreciate
assistance in eliminating, in future
editions, any accurate dates or
undistorted facts that may
have insinuated them-
selves despite the
most painstaking
research and
proofread-
ing.
R.A.

APOLOGIA.

THE AUTHOR APOLOGIZES FOR BEING UNABLE
TO AFFORD A GHOST WRITER, WHICH EXPLAINS
THE LACK OF A DISTINCTIVE PROSE STYLE.

CHAPTER I.

THE DISCOVERY OF AMERICA.

AMERICA was founded by Columbus in 1492. This is an easy date to remember because it rhymes with "ocean blue," which was the color of the Atlantic in those days. If he had sailed a year later the date would still be easy to remember because it would rhyme with "boundless sea."

Columbus fled to this country because of persecution by Ferdinand and Isabella, who refused to believe the world was round, even when Columbus showed them an egg. Ferdinand later became famous because he objected to bullfights and said he preferred to smell flowers if he had to smell anything. He was stung in the end by a bee.

Before Columbus reached America, which he named after a man called American Vesuvius, he cried "Ceylon! Ceylon!" because he wanted to see India, which was engraved on his heart, before he died. When he arrived, he cried again. This time he cried "Excelsior!" meaning "I have founded it." Excelsior has been widely used ever since by persons returning with chinaware from China, with indiaware from India, and with underware from Down Under.

Columbus was mistaken in thinking he had reached India when actually he had not got even as far as Indiana. There is still a great deal of confusion about the East and the West. As Columbus discovered, if you go west long enough you find yourself in the east, and vice versa. The East and the West are kept apart by the Date Line, just as the North and

South are kept apart by the Masons' Dixon Line. In the New World most of the eastern half of the country is called the Middle West, although it is known as the East by those who live in the Far West.

Columbus, who was as confused as anybody who has been at sea for a long time, called the first people he saw "Indians." It is not known what they called Columbus. His unfortunate error has been perpetuated through the centuries. The original Americans are still known as "Indians," while all manner of immigrants from England, Ireland, Angora, and Liechtenstein are referred to as "Americans." [1]

Accompanied by his devoted followers, the Knights of Columbus, Columbus made several other voyages in search of India. Try as he might, however, he kept discovering America, and finally returned to Spain to die. He lived for a time in Madrid, but spent his last days in Disgrace.

A MINORITY OPINION.

Some say it was not Columbus who discovered America but a man named Leaf Ericson. Leaf came from one of the Scandi-

Leaf Ericson.

navian countries with a shipload of people, all of whom were called Yon Yonson or Ole Olson or Big Swede, and went straight to Wisconsin, where he unloaded his passengers and went back for more.

[1] Or, by their mathematically inclined friends, "100 percent Americans."

On his next trip he went to Minnesota.

We know all this from some undecipherable remarks he made on a piece of stone. This stone has since become an utter rune.

FURTHER EXPLORATIONS.

After Columbus proved the world was round, a great many people went around it. Marco Polo, who was one of the earlier explorers, had the misfortune to live several centuries before Columbus. Therefore, although he got around a good deal, he did not get completely around. He went far to the north, however, and is remembered for his discovery of the Polo regions.

Sir Francis Drake.

The chief rivals in exploration were England and Spain. England had men like Cabot, who spoke only to a man named Lowell, and Sir Francis Drake, who had a singed beard and a ship called the *Golden Behind*.

Nor should we forget Sir Martin Fourflusher.[1]

The struggle between England and Spain came to a climax in an epic sea battle off the Azores known as the Last Fight of the Revenge. In this decisive conflict, Sir Richard Grenville and Alfred Lord Tennyson proved conclusively that the lighter English warships could get more miles to the galleon.

England has ruled the waves ever since and has kept the sun

[1] A direct descendant of the early Saxons, who knew all the Angles.

3

from setting anywhere on her empire, thus providing a longer working day than in other countries.

Other explorers included Bilbo, Cabbage de Vaca, Cortez (known as The Stout, who traveled much in realms looking for gold), and Pantsy de Lion, a thirsty old man who was looking for a drinking fountain.[1] He never found it, but he founded Florida, to which a great many thirsty old men have gone ever since.

Pantsy de Lion.

CHAPTER II.

THE VIRGINIA COLONY.

ALL this time there was not much happening in the New World, except that it was steadily growing older.

This period, known as the Doldrums, came to an end in fifteen-something-or-other when Sir Walter Raleigh, a man with a pointed beard and a pointless way of muddying his cloak, established a colony in America in the hope of pleasing the Queen, whose favor he had been in but was temporarily out of.

[1] Some historians say that in his wanderings through the South he invented the Dixie cup, just in case.

4

Although he claimed the new land in the name of Elizabeth, he called it Virginia, which aroused suspicions in Elizabeth's mind and caused her to confine Sir Walter in a tower. While imprisoned, Sir Walter made good use of his time by writing a history of the world on such scraps of paper as he could find, and filling other scraps of paper with a weed brought back from Virginia.

Sir Walter lost his head.

He had barely completed his history when he lost his head. Had he been permitted to keep it a few years longer he might have become the first man to roll a cigarette with one hand.

The Virginia Colony was lost for a time, and its name was changed to The Lost Colony, but it was subsequently found at about the place where it was last seen. Its original name of Virginia was restored because Elizabeth no longer cared, being dead.[1]

THE INDIANS.

The people who were already in the New World when the white men arrived were the first Americans, or America Firsters. They were also referred to as the First Families of Virginia.

The early colonists found the Indians living in toupees, or wigwams, and sending up smoke signals, or wigwags, with piece

[1] The end of Elizabeth is known as the Elizabethan Period.

pipes. Apparently because of a shortage of pipes, they sat in a circle and passed one pipe around, each biting off a piece as it passed. The chief Indian was named Hiawatha, and his squaw, whose name was Evangeline, did all the work. This was later to become an Old American Custom.

The Chiefs, it must be said in all fairness, were too busy to work. They were engaged in making wampum, or whoopee, when they were not mixing war paint or scattering arrowheads about, to be found centuries later.

In order to have their hands free to work, the squaws carried their babies, or cabooses, on their back, very much as kangaroos carry their babies on their front, only different.

The Indians were stern, silent people who never showed their feelings, even while being scalped. They crept up on their enemies without breaking a twig and were familiar with all the warpaths. Despite their savage ways, they sincerely loved peace, and were called Nobel Savages.

Nobel savages.

Their favorite word was "How," which the colonists soon learned was not a question.

The whites feared the redskins and considered them the forest's prime evil. Some went so far as to say that "The only good Indian is a wooden Indian." The redskins resented the whiteskins because they thought they had come to take their lands away from them, and their fears were well grounded.

6

Captain John Smith was the first of a long line of Smiths who came to this country to keep up with the Joneses.

He was captured by the great Indian Chief, Powhatan, and was about to be killed when Popocatepetl, the fiery young daughter of the Chief, stepped in. We are not told what she stepped in, but she saved Captain John Smith's life, for which he thanked her. Later she married an Englishman, which improved relations.

CHAPTER III.

THE PILGRIMS.

THE PILGRIMS were a branch of the Puritans, and were proud of their family tree.[1] They wore tall hats, which they had to

The Low and High Church.

take off when they went inside because they attended a low church. This displeased King James, who raised the roof. He demanded that they attend the same church as he did. At least

---

[1] These, it should be noted, were the first Puritans. The last Puritan was a Spanish nun named Santa Anna.

7

this is his side of the story, which became known as the King James Version.

Although the King insisted, the Puritans, who were very stiff-necked from years of wearing truffles on their collars, stubbornly declined. They would probably still be declining if they had not left England and gone to Leyden, a city in Holland noted for the discovery of electricity in a jar. (Electricity was subsequently lost for a while, but was rediscovered, by accident, when Benjamin Franklin was told to go fly a kite, and did. See below.)

While in Holland, the Pilgrims suffered from pangs of sin,[1] and sent their children to Dutch Reform Schools when they misbehaved. These children, naturally enough, became Protestants, but their protests were ignored.

THE PLYMOUTH COLONY.

After several years in Holland, the Pilgrims decided to set out for the New World. This decision to move is known as Pilgrims' Progress.

The ship on which they sailed was the *Mayflower*. In stormy weather the women and children descended below the heaving decks, thus becoming the *Mayflower* descendants. There they huddled with the Colonial Dames and other early settlers and passed the weary hours comparing genealogies.

It was a long and perilous voyage across the Atlantic. Several times they were blown off their course. But finally, in 1620, which was a doubly Memorable Year because it was also the year in which they set sail, they sighted the rocky coast. The rock on which they landed they called Plymouth Rock because it reminded them of another rock of the same name in England. They built a small picket fence around it and made it a national shrine.

The first four men ashore became our fourfathers.

THE FIRST WINTER.

After a short stay on Plymouth Rock, which was windy and damp, the Pilgrims sought a more sheltered place to build a

[1] Some years later a man named Sigmund Fraud claimed they enjoyed it.

town. One party went in one direction and one went in another. This was the beginning of the two-party system. When the two parties met, they held the first town meeting.

The first winter was cold,[1] which was a distinct surprise to the Pilgrims. Indeed, they might not have survived but for the corn that was given them by friendly Indians. By a curious quirk of history, it has since become illegal for white men to give Indians either corn or rye.

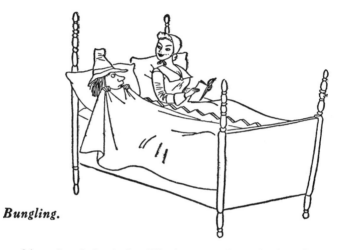

Bungling.

One thing that helped the Pilgrims get through the winter was the economical practice of putting young men and women into bed together, fully clothed. This odd practice, known as bungling, was endured by the young people of the colony until the weather became milder and a sufficient supply of bed-warmers could be imported from England.

The next spring the crops were good, and in the fall the Pilgrims celebrated their first Thanksgiving, which fell, that fall, on a Thursday. The friendly Indians were invited, and the unfriendly Indians stayed in the background, muttering.

[1] Probably responsible for the blue noses which became one of the Pilgrims' outstanding features.

One of the leaders of the little band [1] at Plymouth was Captain Miles Standish. He was known throughout the township for his courtship.

He was an exceptional man. Except for him, almost all the Pilgrims were named William or John. One of the latter was Miles Standish's friend, quiet John Alden, a man who did not speak for himself until spoken to. He was spoken to, and sharply, by the fair Priscilla, whom he married, much to the annoyance of Miles Standish, who thought he was stood up by his stand-in.

———◆———

CHAPTER IV.

THE COLONIES GROW.

LET US leave the Pilgrims in Plymouth and see what was happening elsewhere in New England.

Education took a forward step with the founding of Harvard in a yard near the Charles River. Among the early benefactors of Harvard was a plantation owner from the South known as "Cotton" Mather. The first library was only a five-foot shelf, given to the college by T. S. Eliot, a graduate who no longer had need of it.[2] The books on this shelf are known as the Great Books and have grown to one hundred.

With the founding of two other old colleges, Old Eli and Old Nassau, the educational system was complete. Because of the ivory towers which were a distinctive feature of many of the early buildings, the three colleges became known as the Ivory League.

To provide recreational facilities for students at Harvard, the city of Boston was established. Boston became famous for its two famous hills, Beacon and Bunker, its two famous

---

[1] A precursor of such bandleaders as Paul Whiteman and Benny Goodman.
[2] Having made a fortune in real estate by the sale of wasteland.

churches, North and South, and its two famous bays, Back and Front.

The people of Boston became wealthy by exporting baked beans and codfish, which they were smart enough not to eat themselves. Many, who were pillars of the church and pillars of society, came to be known as Propper Bostonians.

WILLIAMS AND PENN.

One who was unhappy with life in Plymouth was Roger Williams, who thought the Pilgrims were intolerable. The Pilgrims, in turn, thought Williams was impossible. He proposed that they pay the Indians for their land instead of simply taking it from them. This utopian suggestion was dismissed by the Pilgrims as economically unsound.

Roger Williams' reluctant departure.

Because of his unorthodox views, the Pilgrims branded him. They branded him a heretic, and drove him from town to town, although he preferred to walk. This was why Roger Williams reluctantly left Plymouth and founded Rhode Island, which is really not an island and is so small that it is usually indicated on maps by the letters "R.I." out in the Atlantic Ocean. It was once densely wooded. It is now densely populated.[1]

William Penn, on the other hand, came to America to collect some land the King owed his father. He belonged to a frightened religious sect known as the Quakers. So that he would not be

---

[1] Many, with leftist political leanings, became Rhode Island Reds.

forgotten, he gave his name to the Pennsylvania Railroad, the Pennsylvania Station, and the state prison, which is known as the Penn.

MASSACHUSETTS BAY.

The English had always been a seafaring race, ever since they were Danes. Therefore one of their first acts in the New World was to make Massachusetts Bay a colony. From Massachusetts Bay and the nearby bayous they went out in their high-masted vessels looking for whale oil, which they found mostly in whales. The men who went away on voyages to capture whales were called whalers. So, by coincidence, were their sturdy ships. This is more confusing to us now than it was then.

The most famous whale, in those days, was an ill-tempered, unpredictable old whale called Moody Dick. Everyone was on the lookout for him, especially whalers whose legs he had bitten off in one of his nastier moods. The one-legged whaler who was most resentful was Captain A. Hab, who persisted until he finally managed to harpoon Moody Dick where it hurt the most. The whale had the last word, however, for he overturned Captain A. Hab's ship, the *Peapod*, which went down with all hands, including both of Captain A. Hab's.

Thomas Hooker.

12

Fortunately for those who liked to visit New York (see below) but preferred not to live there, Connecticut was founded within commuting distance.

It was founded by Thomas Hooker, a clergyman who, in a dim church, interpreted the Gospel according to his own lights. He would also accept no money for his preaching, which set a low wage standard for others; he was therefore scorned as a free thinker. So he left under a cloud. Many of his parishioners believed his stern words about hell and followed him to Hartford, where he guaranteed them protection in the hereafter and sold them the first fire-insurance policies.

Connecticut is usually spelled Conn, which is easier.

CHAPTER V.

LIFE IN OLD NEW ENGLAND.

MOST of the Puritans were ministers. Each week they could hardly wait until Sunday, when they preached for several hours on such subjects as "Hellfire" and "Damnation." In those days, church attendance was as good every Sunday as it is today on Easter.

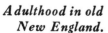
Adulthood in old New England.

All of the Puritans, except a few who should never have left England, were opposed to sin. When a woman sinned, they pinned a scarlet letter "A" on her breast, where it would be conspicuous. Women who won their letter year after year were disdainfully called Scarlet, like Scarlet O'Hara and Scarlet Pimpernel. Children were kept in innocence of the meaning of the "A" and thought it stood for "Adulthood," when such things usually happened.

The homes of the Puritans were simple and austere, but their furniture was antique and therefore frightfully expensive. The chairs were as straight and stiff as the Puritans themselves, and had hard bottoms. They became known as period pieces because they went to pieces after a short period of sitting on them. The women had large chests, or collector's items, of which they were extremely proud. Some of these have been handed down from generation to generation and are displayed proudly by their owners today.

Stores were known as Shoppes, or Ye Olde Shoppes. Prices were somewhat higher at the latter.

The Puritans believed in justice. A woman who was a witch, or a man who was a son of a witch, was punished by being stuck in the stocks. These were wooden devices that had holes to put the arms and legs through, and were considered disgraceful. They were also considered uncomfortable.

Every day the men went out into the fields in their blunder-busses and sowed corn. The women, meanwhile, were busy at

Puritan justice.

home embroidering the alphabet and the date on a piece of cloth. One of the women, Hester Primmer, one of the New England Primmers, never got beyond the first letter of the alphabet. She also had only one date. That was with a young minister and was enough.

Other amusements were pillories, whipping posts, and Indian massacres.

THE LAND.

The land was stony and hilly, except in places where it was hilly and stony. The stones were useful for making millstones and milestones. The Indians sharpened them and used them for scalping and other social purposes.

The hills were useful to watch for Indians from, unless the Indians were already on them. They were hard to plow up, but they were relatively easy to plow down.

THE CLIMATE.

The winters in New England were long. Largely for this reason, the summers were short. In keeping with the seasons, long underwear was worn in the winter and short underwear in the summer.

———◆———

CHAPTER VI.

THE DUTCH AND THE FRENCH COME TO AMERICA.

Many believed there was a shorter way to get to Asia than around America. Not yet having discovered the Panama Canal, they were looking for the next best thing, which was the Northwest Passage. Since it did not exist, it was, of course, hard to find. Nevertheless many Intrepid Explorers made their reputation hunting for it.

One of those who sought the Northwest Passage was Henry

Hudson. In a ship of which he was part owner, called the *Half Mine,* he led a crew of Dutchmen to the mouth of the Hudson River, which he was pleased to find named after himself.

Stopping only to make friends with the Indians and to buy the island of Manhattan from an Indian named Minnehaha (or "Laughing Minnie") for a handful of beads,[1] he pushed on up the river. When he stopped pushing he was in Albany, and he was disappointed. The water was getting shallower and shallower and it was clear. It was clear that this was not the Northwest Passage, and that instead of founding an important route to the Orient, he was about to founder at the state capital. The choice was also clear. He must remain in Albany or make the hard and perilous voyage back across the Atlantic. Without hesitation he chose the latter.

Henry Hudson.

On a second trip to the New World in search of the elusive Passage, Henry Hudson sailed into Hudson Bay. This, again, was not the Northwest Passage, but its name had a familiar ring.

It is not known what became of this Able Navigator who had not been able to find what he was looking for. One theory is that

[1] Beads were then selling at $24 a handful.

Hudson met Cadillac and De Soto, and that together they discovered Detroit.

NEW AMSTERDAM.

Because of Henry Hudson's explorations, the Dutch laid claim to the mouth of the Hudson River, which in their systematic way they divided into the North River and the East River. A stubborn race, they named Manhattan New Amsterdam, although it was obviously New York.

Poltroons.

New Amsterdam was soon swarming with wealthy Dutch traitors known as poltroons. These were bluff, hearty men who smoked long pipes and loved to eat burghers. They frequently had their pictures painted, and one of the most picturesque was their Governor, Rip Van Wrinkle, a one-legged gentleman who fell into a deep sleep while watching a bowling game.

The English also claimed Manhattan, in view of the fact that the beads with which it was purchased were plainly stamped "Made in England." The Dutch could not see the merits of their claim, but they could see that the English had more guns on their warships, so they left.

This was a turning point.

The clever English changed the name Amsterdam to York, but they retained the New.[1]

[1] The city was later called New York, New York, for the sake of those who did not catch it the first time.

The French, although exhausted by the Hundred Years' War, were not too tired to try to establish themselves in the New World. There were still mountains which had not been planted with flags, and there were still rivers that had not been sailed up. So they sailed up them. Many of these still rivers ran deep and led into fastnesses where no white man had ever trod and very few had walked.

At last the only river remaining to be sailed up was the Mississippi. In this instance the French explorer La Salle defied convention. A headstrong young man, he began at the headwaters of the mighty river and sailed down it. He thus not only opened up a vast new territory but discovered an easier means of navigating the rivers of America. La Salle's interesting account of his trip down the river, called *Life on the Mississippi*, is available in an English translation by Mark Twain.

Thanks to La Salle, the Mississippi basin remained in French hands until they grew tired of holding it and sold it for $15,000,000, which many thought was a high price for a second-hand basin.

It is to the French also that we owe the establishment of the beautiful city of Quebec, which was named, according to custom, after the King of France, whose name, according to custom, was Louis (pronounced kwĕ-bĕk'). The English later

The English dominated the French.

seized Quebec and its outskirts, called Canada, from the French, but not without a struggle.

Henceforth the French were dominated by the English, who became our Good Neighbors to the north. We have had amicable relations ever since by agreeing that there are two sides to everything, for example Niagara Falls, which has an American side and a Canadian side.

FIRST TEST.

1. Why do you think Columbus was so interested in traveling to distant places? What else do you know about his home life?

2. Are you really convinced that the world is round? Do you worry much about it?

3. To what extent would the course of American history have been altered if America had never been discovered?

4. What would you say about the Puritans? Would you say the same if they were listening?

5. Can the passengers on the *Mayflower* be considered immigrants? With their strong sense of duty, do you suppose they tried to conceal anything from the customs officials?

6. Have you ever thought how much of a Pilgrim was wasted when an Indian kept only his scalp?

7. Trace on a map the voyages of Henry Hudson. Use a solid line to show where he went and a dotted line to show where he thought he was going. Sign on the dotted line.

8. What would you have done if you had been in La Salle's shoes? How do you know he wore any?

CHAPTER VII.

BEGINNINGS OF THE AMERICAN REVOLUTION.

MOST of the people in the American colonies at this time were English, as were the people in England, who were older because England was the mother country.

As a result of costly wars with the French and Indians, England found herself in need of money. The King, who was George III for a long time, thought of taxing postage stamps used by the colonists. This tax was to be only on outgoing letters, however, and is not to be confused with the income tax, which was a later development.

A spirited address.

Nevertheless the colonists objected. They met clandestinely in taverns and made many spirited addresses. Watchwords such as "Death and Taxes" were on every lip, both upper and lower.

The colonists were further enraged because, even if they paid taxes on their stamps, they would have no representatives in Parliament, which had only M.P.s.[1] Tempers were at the breaking point. The situation was grave, even serious.

THE BOSTON TEA PARTY.

The colonists, who were now called Americans, which was only fair in view of what the British were being called, tried to

[1] Military Police.

21

avoid the stamp tax by writing fewer and fewer letters. They became Bad Correspondents. This made the King mad,[1] so mad that he thought up a diabolical scheme of forcing the Americans to drink tea instead of coffee. This led to the first act of violence.

A storm of protest swept Boston. Many Bostonians actually preferred tea, but they objected to being told what to drink, especially by a King three thousand miles away who had never gone to Harvard.

The Boston Tea Party.

A shipload of tea was then in Boston Harbor. This was too much for the good people of Boston. Half a shipload, in fact, would have been sufficient. Disguising themselves as Indians, they crept across Boston Harbor and clambered up the side of the anchored ship. There, armed with knives and war hoops, they quickly subdued the crew and threw tea bag after tea bag into the water. Then they crept back across the harbor and returned to their homes, where they rebelliously drank coffee.

---

[1] Ironically enough, George III died insane. It is an interesting commentary on American history, not hitherto noted by any historian, that every British sovereign since George III has also died,[2] except the present one.

[2] The sole exception to the historical principle formulated above is King Edward VIII, who not only married an American but, when last seen in New York, was still alive.

The British suspected that the Indians were really Americans but they could not be sure without seeing the whites of their eyes. The Americans, employing a method of disguise later popular in Hollywood, wore dark glasses.[1]

As coming events were to disclose, this was no mere prank but a Blow for Freedom. Although humorously called the Boston Tea Party, it is more correctly referred to as the Boston Massacre, or, in its abbreviated form, Boston Mass.

THE CONTINENTAL CONGRESS.

The King (who was still George III) stubbornly persisted in his plan to tax the American colonists, whom he considered upstarts, pipsqueaks, and rabble rousers. Since the Americans did not like to be thought of in these terms, they held secret meetings in such unexpected places as Faneuil Hall and the belfry of Old South Church, and thought up one or two terms for the King. A conservative faction was opposed to more than two terms.

One of the most memorable meetings was that known as the First Continental Congress. Among the leaders at this meeting were Samuel and John Adams, who were cousins, and Patrick and Henry, whose last name has been forgotten but who were probably brothers, since everyone was closely related in those days. Sam Adams was born with a silver spoon in his mouth, but once it was removed he became a fine orator. A generous man, he made an Important Contribution.

Patrick and Henry were even more influential. Despite the fact that they had been in business in a country store and had failed, they were highly successful in public affairs. Such success stories came to be a commonplace in the 19th and 20th centuries, owing largely to writings by Ralph Waldorf Emerson and Horatio Algae on behalf of ragged individualism.

Patrick and Henry often arose in meetings, such as the Continental Congress, and spoke as with a single voice. Their speeches were invariably rousing. Once they called the King a

[1] Had the British used similar cunning at Bunker Hill, the course of history might have been altered.

23

Tyrant and a Despot, and were wildly applauded. This was Dangerous Talk. Another time they rose to oratorical heights and delivered a speech that was long remembered, even after the meeting was over. It was the famous Battle Cry of the Republic, reaching its climax in a forthright demand for better clothing for the colonists, "Give us livery, or give us death!" The audience was deeply moved, although some remained in their seats until it was time for the Second Continental Congress, which followed immediately.

The die was cast. The American Revolution would have begun then, but it was not yet 1776.

CHAPTER VIII.

THE AMERICAN REVOLUTION.

ONE last effort to avoid the American Revolution was made by a friendly Englishman. He was Edmund Burke, the author of

Burke's plea.

Burke's Works. Although he did not believe in giving the colonies their independence, he was in favor of reconciliation.[1]

[1] Later called appeasement.

His speeches on behalf of the colonies were so long and loud that they were called oratorios. In one of these, he pleaded with the King to lift the tax burden from the colonists and put it back on the English, who were accustomed to it. But by the time Burke had finished speaking the King was an old man and had become hard of hearing. Thus Burke's plea fell on deaf ears.

CONCORD AND LEXINGTON.

By various means, such as the grapevine, the underground, and the subway, the British learned that the Americans were collecting powder in a room in Concord. A detachment of British soldiers was therefore detached, although not without difficulty, from Boston, and sent with orders to break into the powder room. The whole country was scandalized.

Paul Revere.

Fortunately for the Americans, they had been forewarned. Although hardly a man is now alive who remembers the entire poem that was written about his exploits, Paul Revere got up at midnight and awakened everyone with his cries. He had seen a light in the steeple of Old North Church, and knew at once that the British were coming by land or sea. Accompanied by William Dawes,[1] he carried the news from Boston to Concord

[1] Who, unfortunately, had an inferior press agent and thus did not go down in history.

25

and from Ghent to Aix. When dawn broke, the countryside swarmed with countrymen.

At Lexington, the British found a little band of Americans playing in the town square and shouted to them to disband. This was the "shout that was heard round the world." Loud as it was, the Americans pretended not to hear, and the British marched on to Concord, still shouting. There they met a larger band of Americans and the same thing happened except that shouts were exchanged, and the rate of exchange was unfavorable to the British, who thought it advisable to return to Boston. As they marched down the road, rolling their drums in front of them, the Americans hid behind trees, bushes, and billboards and derisively shouted "Redcoats" and "Reds" at the British, who were humiliated.

BUNKER HILL.

Smarting under their defeat, the British began a series of intolerable acts. One of these was to quarter [1] colonists who failed to cooperate. Another was to raid military stores, where the thrifty merchants were selling Army surplus.

A Minute Man.

The colonists fought back with muskets (which they kept hanging on the nearest wall), pitchforks (with which they fought pitched battles), and teeth and nails of various sizes. They were always ready to fight within an hour, which is why they were called Minute Men.

[1] The British never did anything by halves.

26

One of the first battles took place at Bunker Hill, where a tall monument afforded an excellent view of Boston and the surrounding countryside. Although the Americans were finally driven from this strategic point, they proved their courage and marksmanship by firing only at the whites of eyes, disdaining any larger target. The British, despite having a superior force of major generals, knew they had met a Worthy Foe.

GEORGE WASHINGTON.

It was time for the colonists to have a leader, and who better than George Washington? He had all the desired qualifications, to wit:

(1) He was widely known, since everyone had seen his picture on stamps and dollar bills.

(2) He was a person of social standing, being a country gentleman with a large estate which was open to the public on Sundays.

(3) He was a man of great physical strength, having chopped down a cherry tree when he was a small boy.

(4) He cared nothing for money, on one occasion having thrown a silver dollar across a river.

(5) His birthday, which would be a holiday if he became famous, came in February, which at that time was badly in need of holidays.[1]

George Washington was therefore chosen to lead the brave but outnumbered colonists. He took command of his forces under a spreading chestnut tree in Cambridge, after which he returned home only long enough to marry Martha Washington and make preparations to become the father of his country.

[1] It was not known then that Lincoln would also be born in February.

FAMILY TREE* OF GEORGE WASHINGTON.

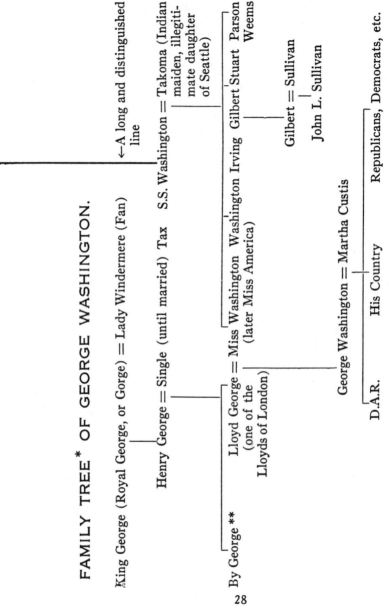

King George (Royal George, or Gorge) = Lady Windermere (Fan) ←A long and distinguished line

Henry George = Single (until married) Tax   S.S. Washington = Takoma (Indian maiden, illegitimate daughter of Seattle)

By George**

Lloyd George = Miss Washington Washington Irving Gilbert Stuart Parson Weems
(one of the   (later Miss America)
Lloyds of London)

Gilbert = Sullivan

John L. Sullivan

George Washington = Martha Custis

D.A.R.   His Country   Republicans, Democrats, etc.

28

* Cherry, of course.
** Said to be founder of Society for Prevention of Calling Pullman Porters George.

CHAPTER IX.

THE AMERICAN REVOLUTION (CONTINUED).

THE WAR that followed divides itself easily into three periods. These are called, for convenience, the First Period, the Second Period, and the Third Period. They should be kept carefully in mind for a clearer understanding of the following events, each of which is bound to fall in one period or another

SIEGE OF BOSTON.

General Gage and the British were inside the city and wanted to get out. Washington and his men were outside the city and wanted to get in. Both leaders knew this sort of thing could not go on for long. It was a question of nerve. Fortunately for America, General Gage had less than Washington. He soon lost heart, as well as nerve, and sailed for England, which he preferred to Boston anyhow.

CROSSING OF THE DELAWARE.

In order to save British lives, Lord Charles Cornwallis hired several regiments of German Hushians from Germantown. These were quiet, soft-spoken soldiers except when they were roaring drunk, as they were inclined to be at places like Brandywine. With the help of the mercenary Germans, who received pay rather than medals, Cornwallis threw Washington across

The Hushians at Brandywine.

the Delaware River. Washington, however, was not injured, and decided upon a Bold Stroke. Leaving his campfires burning, because he expected to be back shortly, he swiftly recrossed the storm-tossed Delaware in a small boat. Hazardous as it was, Washington stood up during the rough crossing in order that his portrait might be painted by a famous artist in an accompanying boat. Cornwallis could not match Washington; the best English portrait painters were in England, busy painting Lord Nelson, Lady Hamilton, and their Blue Boy.

VALLEY FORGE.

Along with his successes, Washington suffered reverses. Many of the places at which he failed are now commemorated with signs that read, "Washington Slipped Here." His darkest hour, and also his coldest, came at Valley Forge. As he told his friend Tom Paine, who had brought him a new pair of boots, these were the times to try men's soles. For days he trudged about in the snow looking downcast and discouraging his men. Little did he know, because he was several miles inland, that the tide was turning.

A TRAITOR AND A HERO.

Benedict Arnold, though at first thought a well-born American, was ultimately found to be a dastard. He tried to turn West Point, which was then a fort, over to the British. Had he succeeded, he would doubtless have done the same with Annapolis. The plot was discovered, however, when Major John André, the British messenger, stuffed Arnold's message in his boot and developed a limp. André was hanged, and Benedict Arnold took to the high seas and changed his name to Edward Everett Hale, The Man Without a Country.

To vindicate the family name, Nathan Hale, who was on the American side and thus a good spy, went to his death bravely when he was caught by the British. He cheerfully remarked that he wished he could be hanged more often for his country. Benedict Arnold, as we have seen, refused to be hanged even once, which was niggardly and disloyal.

Most of the war was fought on land, but there were a few important battles at sea, owing to demands from the Navy. Chief among our naval heroes was John Paul Jones, who is well remembered. At least he is better remembered than if his name had been merely John Jones. He commanded a stout vessel named the *Bonjour Richard*. It was he who, after his ship was sunk, declared, "I have just begun to fight." He was a brave man, but slow to anger.

*John Paul Jones,
slow to anger.*

FOREIGN AID.

For a time the colonists fought without allies, which was at least better than fighting with them. Foreign shipowners being afraid of England's sea power, almost nothing could be imported in foreign bottoms, and domestic bottoms were all rust and barnacles. The outlook was dim. The issue hung in the balance.

After a while, however, the valiant colonies began to look like a Good Risk, and several first-class powers came to their aid. Had they delayed much longer, America might have won without their help, which would have been embarrassing. Germany sent Baron Steuben and France sent Lafayette. When Lafayette arrived, he declared, "I am here." He did not want to be overlooked. Poland, having no barons or officers handy, sent Ostroski and Wojukowitz, whose progeny have been distinguishing themselves at left guard [1] and right halfback ever since.

YORKTOWN: THE LAST BATTLE.

Feeling between Cornwallis and Washington had grown tense, and the stage was now set for the final act. This came at Yorktown with the unexpected suddenness which one learns to expect at the end of wars. Cornwallis was hemmed in and was unable to extricate himself. After an agonizing struggle, he gave up like a soldier and gentleman.[2] On hearing the news of the surrender of the British, King George (still the III), who had been half mad for some time, went wholly mad and shouted "Let them eat cake!" Henceforth the British were required to send diplomats to America, when they needed funds, instead of tax collectors.

CHAPTER X.

THE FOUNDING FATHERS.

OUR COUNTRY owes a great deal to its founding fathers. These were a group of parents who were determined that their children should have the advantages which they themselves had been denied. One of these advantages, coveted by children ever since, was the opportunity of going to school, which is why schools all over America are named after one or another of the founding fathers, *viz.*, Thomas Jefferson High School, Alexander Hamilton Grammar School, and P.S. 127.

THOMAS JEFFERSON.

Thomas Jefferson is best known as the author of the Declaration of Independence, which is responsible for two holidays,

[1] Not to be confused with the Old Guard.

[2] Lord Cornwallis, handing his sword to General Washington, is reported to have said, "Good show, old boy." This expression is untranslatable.

July Fourth and Declaration Day. Although he was the author of this important document, he failed to secure a copyright, and it was therefore signed by a great many persons, including Charles Carroll of Carrollton, a high-stepper named Francis Lightfoot Lee, and a slovenly fellow called Unbuttoned Gwinnett, all of whom became known as signers, co-signers, or tangents. These men signed in such space as was left them by John Hancock, who had taken a course in penmanship and was still practicing.

Unbuttoned Gwinnett.

It was also Jefferson, an exceedingly handy man with tools, who framed the Declaration of Independence and hung it on the wall of the Library of Congress, where it may be observed today by those interested in seeing John Hancock's John Hancock.

Jefferson was not only a statesman but an inventor. His many inventions include the dumb-waiter, the decimal system of coinage (enabling us to make change, which is still impossible in England), the swivel chair, the University of Virginia, and the Democratic Party.[1] An extremely versatile person, he was also an architect, thus saving a fee when he built his home.

[1] The Democrats first called themselves Republicans, to distinguish themselves from the Federalists. When the Federalists discovered how successful the Democrats were as Republicans, they decided to become Republicans too. To preserve the two-party system, the original Republicans generously became Democrats, and let the new Republicans have Lincoln, which was a serious error.

More equal than others.

Deeply religious, Jefferson was for a time a minister to France. In his spare time, he was a farmer and an aristocrat.

Jefferson made a great contribution to American political philosophy. He believed that all men are created equal, but that some are created more equal than others.

ALEXANDER HAMILTON.

It is a little-known fact that Alexander Hamilton was born in the West Indies. It is also of little importance. Hamilton became known as the best Secretary of the Treasury until Andrew Mellon. Both he and Mellon, it should be noted, were helped by the fact that the country enjoyed good times during their terms of office. This is always a good thing for a Secretary of the Treasury.

Hamilton, a reactionary, was opposed to debt. In order to pay the costs of the war against the British, he established a mint. It was the sale of mint, for mint juleps, to army officers from the South, that put the new government on its feet and removed a good many Southern colonels from theirs. Hamilton also instituted a system of taxes, which the people of America accepted willingly as soon as Hamilton assured them he was not British.

Because he was a Federalist and Jefferson was a Republican (Democrat), Hamilton and Jefferson never saw eye to eye, which caused considerable strain. Hamilton supported the businessman and Jefferson supported the farmer. This was generous of them, but they were both well able to afford it.

Just before the end of his life, Hamilton engaged in a duel with Aaron Burr, a disappointed presidential candidate who never got beyond the vice-presidency. It is not known whether Burr shot (1) straighter or (2) sooner, but (3) he was declared the winner, and Hamilton, his time being up, (4) expired. One of the unanswered questions of history is why the ambitious Burr shot Hamilton instead of Jefferson, which would have given him the presidency. It would, however, have established a bad precedent for vice-presidents.

BENJAMIN FRANKLIN.

As a boy, Benjamin Franklin helped his father make candles, which were thought to look more romantic than electric lights. Later his father apprenticed him to a printer, and Benjamin became a printer's devil, much to the printer's dismay.

He was self-educated, which means that he was too poor to go to school and therefore got a good education.

When he was twelve, Benjamin became so interested in reading that he gave up eating in order to buy books. A few months later, his appetite getting the better of him, he ran away to Philadelphia, where he sold his books and thereafter walked around with an enormous loaf of bread under each arm.

In between trips to the bakery, young Franklin was hard at work flying kites, putting up lightning rods, discovering electricity, and thinking up wise sayings like "A penny saved is the best policy" and "Early to bed and early to rise keeps the dark circles from under your eyes." These sayings he contributed to *Poor Richard's Almanack,* which published them because he was the owner. He printed this periodical by hand, since he could never learn to do it with his feet.

Franklin was a plump, well-rounded man who invented almost as many things as Jefferson, including silkworms, whisk brooms, the Franklin stove, and bifocals. As Postmaster General, he instituted general delivery, and also established the dead-letter office, a place for keeping letters from people who

*Franklin
discovering
electricity.*

were deceased. He also made it possible for congressmen to send their letters free, which later became known as the Franklin Privilege.

When Franklin was seventy, he was sent to Paris to see what he could do to improve relations with the French, and he is said to have done extremely well despite his age. He died full of honors, *escargots, pâté,* and *vin rouge.*

◆

CHAPTER XI.

THE NEW NATION.

ONE of the key points in the peace treaty with England was the agreement not to fight another war until 1812. This gave America what is known as a Breathing Spell. As a result of this, Americans took in a lot of fresh air and became chesty, vastly improving the appearance of young women who were later to become the heroines of historical novels.

There was much discussion about what to call the new nation. Some wanted to call it merely The Nation, others preferred

Heroines of historical novels.

the New Republic. Those who believed in States' Rights insisted on the Untied States. Those who supported Labor wanted it called the Union. It was finally decided, as the result of what is known as the XYZ Affair, to call it the U.S.A., the U.S., or, when one is abroad, The States. The U.S.A. was the first of a long series of alphabetical agencies which reached an impasse in the time of F.D.R., when the alphabet was exhausted.

THE FLAG.

The first flag of the United States was made by Betsy Ross, assisted by Molly Pitcher (a little woman who had big ears), Barbara Frietchie, and other members of the Philadelphia Sewing Circle. In the original flag there were thirteen stars, but since many persons were superstitious, more stars were quickly added.

THE CONSTITUTION.

The thrifty English had an unwritten constitution, which saved them a large printing bill. But the Americans decided to write theirs out in order to have something for the Supreme Court to interpret.

The Constitution provided for the following:

1. Two houses, a lower and an upper, with a stairway, or escalator clause, between. Bills, which were afterwards to be sent to taxpayers for collection, would first be thrown into a large hopper and allowed to age. Members of the lower house were to be elected according to population—that is, according to whether enough of the population voted for them. Members of the upper house were to represent the states instead of the people. To get into the upper house, it was necessary to have:

(*a*) A broad-brimmed hat

(*b*) A flowing bow tie

(*c*) A good name

(*d*) A key or a ladder

2. Congressional immunity: a special health program under which senators were inoculated against lawsuits.

3. A system of checks and balances, which led to the national debt.

4. Committees: smaller groups which killed bills, tabled proposals, played poker, and generally ran things.

THE FIRST AND SECOND PRESIDENTS.

George Washington was the first president. He might have stayed in office for life, but he wanted to get out for some fresh air.[1] Furthermore, he had prepared an eloquent farewell address, which he was impatient to deliver.

He was followed, at a respectful distance, by John Adams. Although Adams was the second president, he was the first vice-president, and this was some consolation.

THE NEW CAPITAL.

The capital (which is spelled capitol when it is the building and not the city or vice versa) was first New York City, but since all of the presidents came from Virginia, commuting was a problem. It was therefore moved to Washington, which

[1] He also wanted to go back to the farm. In this, Washington set a precedent. Almost every figure in American public life has expressed a desire to go back to the farm, even when he didn't come from one.

Adams followed Washington.

was called Washington, D.C., to differentiate it from Washington, George.

CHAPTER XII.

DIFFICULTIES OF THE NEW GOVERNMENT.

In its first years, the United States was visited by trials and tribulations. United in war, the new nation was now torn by dissension and tormented by doubt. The Minute Men had grown old, and were taking longer. The Navy consisted chiefly of the Ship of State, which many considered unseaworthy. As if all this were not bad enough, our presidents failed to measure up to Washington, who was a very tall man.

ALIEN AND SEDUCTION ACTS.

Among the ill-advised laws passed by the new government were the Alien and Seduction Acts, which gave foreigners the choice of either ceasing their acts of seduction or becoming citizens. These laws were soon repealed, however, when it was found that seduction was also practiced by native-born citizens.

39

*The Alien and
Seduction Act.*

WHISKY REBELLION.

Another unwise act was perpetrated when the government
sent its officials to collect a tax from farmers who were allowing
their grain to stand in the fields until it spoiled and turned into
whisky. Since it was hard to reach the outlying farms, owing to
unpaved roads, this was called the Exercise Tax. The farmers
objected to paying such a tax and said they would drink their
own whisky first, which some of them courageously did. The
entire country was in a ferment. A force of militiamen[1] was
sent against the rebellious farmers, who sobered up when they
saw they were outnumbered. The whisky was seized by the
Federalists. This practice of taking over spoiled grain, known
as the Spoils System, lost the Federalists the farm vote at the
next election, as well as the support of the WCTU, which believed that confiscated whisky should be poured down the drain
instead of down the hatch.

INDECISION.

Unable to wait for the next war with the United States, England was at this time at war with France, which was closer
anyhow. The United States considered entering the war also, but
could not decide which country would win. Throughout the

[1] Soldiers who had taken the Pledge.

war it remained undecided, or neutral, and looked around for a smaller country to fight.

This opportunity came unexpectedly when a band of Barbarian Pirates, or Coarse Hairs, seized one of our ships and took it into the port of Tripoli, one of the Barbarian States in North Africa. The Bad Shaw of Tripoli, insulted by the smallness of the bribe he was offered, declared war on the United States. The United States was in turn insulted, thinking that it should have been permitted to declare war first.

In the war that followed, none of the admirals received as much publicity as Lieutenant Stephen Decatur, who daringly rowed into the harbor of Tripoli and afterwards rowed out again, despite the fact that the Coarse Hairs had batteries all along the shore and turned the current against him. This heroic exploit did not end the war, however, which dragged on until we finally made a Bold Move. We caught the enemy by surprise, on the shores of Tripoli, by making a landing with our Marines, who came on the run from the halls of Montezuma.

The Bad Shaw declared war.

41

SECOND TEST.

1. Which of these was most unbearable to the colonists:
   (*a*) Taxes?
   (*b*) Tea?
   (*c*) Letter writing?
2. Was King George resentful because he was always third?
3. Why was the year 1776 chosen for the Revolution? Were there any other good years along about then?
4. Look into the mirror. Examine the whites of *your* eyes. What if the Redcoats at Bunker Hill had been suffering from pinkeye?
5. Write a brief essay of twenty-five words or less on "I like George Washington because. . . ." Your answer should be accompanied by twenty-five cents and a box top.
6. How would you have dealt with Aaron Burr if you were no better a shot than Alexander Hamilton?
7. Name three inventions which Jefferson and Franklin overlooked. Explain why.
8. Come to some sort of a conclusion.

CHAPTER XIII.

EXPANSION.

ALL this time the population was growing. People were getting larger and larger. Crowded conditions in the Eastern part of the United States, or the East Side, were becoming intolerable. At first people in the East refused to go West, but as the population continued to grow, they finally came to their census. Before long many farmers, who had heard about the fertile lands to the west (or to the left, if a map is being used), shouldered their hoes and set forth, shouting their stirring cry, "Westward Hoes!" A few people from Massachusetts joined the westward movement, but because of their Boston accent they had difficulty making themselves understood west of the Hudson River.[1]

LOUISIANA PURCHASE.

West of the Atlantic seaboard and from Canada to the Gulf of Mexico stretched a vast territory that was owned by a wealthy Frenchman named Napoleon. Even without stretching, it was a large area. It was heavily wooded, having been seeded by the King of Spain some years before.

An inexpensive way of exporting American products from the interior was to send them down the Mississippi River on rafts, riffrafts, log jams, and showboats, piloted by such experienced rivermen as Mark Twain, Mark Time, Mark Hopkins (on one end of a log), Huckleberry Finn, Mickey Finn, and Old Man River. The French controlled New Orleans, however, and thus were able to bottle up the Mississippi, which they did and sold to American tourists.

This situation could not continue. The United States therefore asked Napoleon if he would sell New Orleans, bottling works and all. To everyone's surprise, Napoleon, who was in financial straits because of the lavish tomb he was building

[1] Their broad "A" is not to be confused with the Scarlet Letter.

himself in Paris, accepted the offer and threw in the environs (see Mississippi Basin, above), which stretched northward to Canada and included East St. Louis.

LEWIS N. CLARK.

The region west of the Mississippi was a trackless wilderness, and without tracks railroads were useless. Transportation was therefore extremely slow. To open up this new country and to find such states as Oregon and Washington, which were thought to be out there somewhere, a brave young explorer named Lewis N. Clark was told to go west, which he did.[1]

Lewis N. Clark.

Lewis N. Clark was a trail blazer and a path breaker and a very good man in the bush because he never got poison ivy. He carried beads to give to the Indians, who sewed them on bookmarks, handbags, and watch fobs to sell to tourists at Albuquerque.[2]

Starting from St. Louis, Lewis N. Clark went northwestward until he found the headwaters of the Missouri, and thence to the

[1] The person who told him was probably Horace Greeley, who sent many young men West to die with their boots on. Mr. Greeley died in the East, in bed.

[2] A city in New Mexico, whose name the Indians avoided spelling by refusing to learn to write.

mouth of the Columbia River, where he spent a trying winter. Mostly he was trying to keep warm. The next spring, secure in the knowledge that he was the first white man to reach the Pacific Ocean by the land route, he turned his face homeward. On the way east he saw many huge herds of bison, which he mistakenly called buffalo. But for this error, one of our noted plainsmen (see below) would be known as Bison Bill.

———◆———

CHAPTER XIV.

THE WAR OF 1812.

A SENSIBLY NAMED war was the War of 1812, the date of which can easily be remembered by anyone who can remember its name. The chief causes of the war were the following:

1. The British were then fighting against Napoleon (who had not as yet met his Waterloo at Waterloo) and would not allow our ships to enter French ports. They established blockheads, or port authorities, to see that this edict was enforced.

2. The British claimed the right to search American ships

Hotheads.

45

and take from them any British sailors born on board. Sometimes they took American sailors also, and occasionally the Americans were flattered, or impressed, into helping the British sail their ships.

3. Hotheads like John C. Calhoun and Henry Clay held a war party, at which they entertained all the congressmen and played war games. By the time a considerable amount of firewater had been consumed, there was hardly a cool head left in the government.

NAVAL BATTLES.

The War of 1812 was fought mostly at sea. One of our greatest victories was when the warship *Constitution*, captained by the immortal Barnacle Bill, thundered volley after volley at the British fleet. One of the British ships, a frigid named the *Derrière*,[1] was quickly sent to the bottom. Another victory occurred when Commodore Perry, on his way back from discovering the North Pole, swept the British from Lake Erie. The place has been kept tidy ever since.

BURNING OF WASHINGTON.

A dastardly act of the British was their landing soldiers on the shores of Chesapeake Bay without warning, and then proceeding to burn Washington. Fortunately Dolly Madison, the mistress of the White House, was a woman of great strength and presence of mind. She carried off everything of value, including the Declaration of Independence, the Mint, and the Washington Monument. After the British had gone, she returned everything to its place,[2] thus establishing herself as the most honest public servant until Lincoln.

THE BOMBARDMENT OF FORT MC HENRY.

In an attempt to take Baltimore, the British attacked Fort McHenry, which protected the harbor. Bombs were soon burst-

[1] Which shot only grapes.
[2] See Webster's definition of *dolly*: "a small wheeled truck for moving heavy beams, columns, etc."

ing in air, rockets were glaring, and all in all it was a moment of great historical interest. During the bombardment, a young lawyer named Francis Off Key wrote "The Star-Spangled Banner," and when, by the dawn's early light, the British heard it sung, they fled in terror.

Dolly Madison.

THE BATTLE OF NEW ORLEANS.

General Andrew Jackson, who was on his way to Florida for the winter, heard that the British were going to New Orleans to force their way into the Mardi Gras, to which they had not been invited. After days of hard riding, he reached the city, where he immediately threw up redoubts. Feeling somewhat better, he awaited the British attack. According to custom, the British advanced in a solid line, which our marksmen soon perforated, turned back, and folded under.

Jackson won a great victory and thereby became presidential timber, or Old Hickory. Little did he know that the war had already been over for two weeks and that it was no longer 1812, but 1815.

———◆———

CHAPTER XV.

PRESIDENT MONROE.

James Monroe came from Virginia, the mother of presidents. Little is known of his father, except that he was devoted to Virginia.

Monroe's presidency was a period of much political strife, when everyone enjoyed being angry at everyone else. It was therefore known as the Era of Good Feeling. The Federalists, however, took a dim view of things. In fact they felt so low about losing the election to Monroe that they went underground. Despite a thorough search, no trace has ever been found of them.

The only war at this time was a halfhearted one called the Semi-No War. It came about when General Andrew Jackson chased some Florida Indians into the Everglades, which was their last resort. He also proved to the King of Spain that Florida was not only indefensible but worthless. The King sold it to the United States for a good price and celebrated his shrewd sale by firing a great number of cannons. The noise was deafening and gave rise to the expression, "boom prices."

It was during Monroe's presidency that the Cumberland Road

OKEFENOKEE
ACRES
FISHING - BOATING
FREE BAIT
WATER LOTS

*Jackson
chased the
Florida Indians.*

was built to make it easier to get to Ohio and Illinois. When completed, it was found equally useful in getting *from* Ohio and Illinois, with the result that some weird types began to show up on Broadway and along 42d Street.

MISSOURI COMPROMISE.

Missouri felt left out of things and wanted to join the Union. But it was a slave state (where slaves had to be bought), and was opposed by the free states (where slaves were given away to anyone who wanted them). About the same time, Maine also wanted to join the Union, in order to get Union wages, and of course the slave states objected. This knotty problem was resolved by letting both Missouri and Maine into the Union, thereby making an equal number of persons angry on both sides. This was called the Missouri Compromise and was considered extremely clever by those who thought it up.

MONROE DOCTRINE.

Monroe is best remembered for the Monroe Doctrine. This was fair warning to European nations not to establish any more colonies in America. The United States in turn promised that its colonies in Europe, such as the American colony on the Left Bank, would not make any more trouble.

The chief purpose of the Monroe Doctrine was to protect the new republics in South America from Spain. Shortly afterwards these republics decided they wanted to be protected from the United States.

———◆———

CHAPTER XVI.

THE SECOND ADAMS.

JOHN QUINCY ADAMS was the second Adams to become president. He is not to be confused with his father, John Adams, who was the first Adams but the second president, or with his Uncle

Sam Adams (who was not the real Uncle Sam, except to his nieces and nephews).[1] It was fortunate for us, if not for the second John Adams, that he had the Quincy, which the first John did not.

THE EERIE CANAL.

It was at this time that the Governor of New York, a man of action known as "Do It" Clinton, made a momentous decision. He decided to build a canal from Lake Eerie to the Hudson River in order to bring together the waters of the Great Lakes and the Atlantic Ocean, which he thought should never have

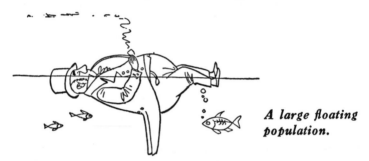

A large floating population.

been separated. People laughed at him and called the canal "Clinton's Big Ditch" and "Do It's Folly," but he lived to laugh at those who laughed at him, and the canal was built. Before long, people from Detroit and Cleveland came barging into New York City, which has had a large floating population ever since.

STEAMSHIPS AND RAILROAD TRAINS.

Steam had already been invented by James What, an inquisitive and observant young fellow who noticed it coming out of a teakettle. By putting two and two and a number of teakettles together, he found he could not only make more tea but press clothes and unseal envelopes.

[1] It becomes all the more confusing when we consider the various Madams Adams.

Transportation was revolutionized by Robert Fulton, who built the first steamboat, and Casey Jones, who invented the steam locomotive. The latter invention led to a number of significant developments that profoundly affected life in America. Chief among these were:

1. Cinders.
2. Windows that could be opened only by someone else.
3. Timetables, with asterisks, daggers, and "Sundays only" in very small type.
4. Railroad tracks, which people lived on the right or wrong side of.

———◆———

CHAPTER XVII.

ANDREW JACKSON SPOILS THE SYSTEM.

ANDREW JACKSON was a popular president. He swore he would shake hands with everyone in town and kept his promise. This delayed the business of his administration for several weeks, until they could take off the bandages. One of the first things President Jackson did, after flexing his fingers, was to reward those who had cast more than one ballot for him by appointing

Jackson shook hands with everyone.

them postmasters, judges, generals, and garbage collectors. It was in this last connection that one of his friends made the famous remark, "To the victors belong the spoils."

NULLIFICATION.

Trouble was caused by South Carolina, an agricultural state, that raised cane over some of Jackson's laws that favored manufacturing states. When South Carolina demanded nullification of these laws, on the grounds that there were enough states already without manufacturing any more, Jackson threatened nullification of South Carolina.

Although nullification was finally nullified, Jackson handled this and other cases so highhandedly that his enemies nicknamed him King Andrew the First, and many wanted to crown him. His friends, however, hailed him as the Great Democrat. This was called an Honest Difference of Opinion.

FURTHER ACCOMPLISHMENTS OF JACKSON.

Jackson is best remembered for having founded the Democratic Party and the Jackson Day Dinner. The latter is a meal where plates are sold for as much as a hundred dollars apiece and are still not supposed to be taken home. The Jackson Day Dinner has grown to be so expensive that only Republicans can afford it.

———◆———

CHAPTER XVIII.

THE BEGINNINGS OF INDUSTRY.

THUS FAR, although people were industrious, there was little industry in America. Smokestacks rarely belched. In cities like Pittsburgh and St. Louis the air was so free of smoke that many persons grew impatient at the lack of progress and disgustedly said they might as well move back to the country. This dearth of industry was largely caused by:

1. A shortage of captains of industry, it being the age of private enterprise.

2. A feeling on the part of some that it was morally wrong to invent things. These persons were mindful of the Biblical saying, "Hell is paved with good inventions."

3. Opposition to change by those who wanted to stop where they were and preferred the *status whoa*.

COTTON GIN.

Industry was furthered at this time by a graduate of Yale, "Old Eli" Whitney. Cotton was causing trouble because it was full of little seeds that had to be picked out by hand, one at a time. Whitney invented a long stick for knocking the seeds out of cotton two or more at a time. This practice came to be known as cotton batting. The far-reaching consequences of progress were immediately apparent: many cottonseed pickers gained additional leisure by being thrown out of work. Whitney also invented a stimulating drink called cotton gin, which enabled one man to do the work of fifty.

THE REAPER.

In the early days, grain was cut with a scythe or sickle by a sickley old man who carried around an hourglass so that he would know when it was quitting time. He was called the Grim Reaper. This slow procedure was speeded up by Cyrus McCormick, familiarly known as Jack the Reaper, who developed a machine with a belt conveyer, which conveyed belts throughout the Middle West and was responsible for establishing the Corn Belt and the Bible Belt.

THE SEWING MACHINE.

Howe, like What, the inventor of the teakettle (see above), was exceedingly curious. He was destined to succeed, because as a young man he lived in a garret. It came to him, in a flash of inspiration, that if McCormick could make a machine that would reap, he should be able to make one that would sew. The only question was Howe, and he answered that for himself.

Communication was improved by S. O. S. Morse, who invented the telegraph and organized the first union of telegraph operators in the West, known as the Western Union. He also developed the secret code that bears his name. Morse's first message on the telegraph was the reverent question, "What hath God wrought?" which is Morse code for "Don't write, telegraph."

———◆———

CHAPTER XIX.

HARD TIMES.

When Martin Van Buren became president, he found government positions for all his supporters. This led to a Great Depression on the part of those who had not supported him. Van Buren was not reelected, but his campaign was so hilarious that he was popularly acclaimed the Panic of 1837.

HARRISON AND TYLER.

Many thought Henry Clay should be the next president, especially the Wigs, a group of bald-headed men who admired his fine head of air. But others felt that Clay, who had said in a speech, "I know no North, no South, no East, no West," was too ignorant to hold such a high office. When he further said, "I would rather be right than be President," the country took him at his word.

William Henry Harrison, who was more careful about stating his preferences, was elected president to succeed Van Buren. John Tyler was elected vice-president on the same ticket. (The ticket read, "Admit W. H. Harrison and Friend.") Their opponents tried desperately to defeat them by circulating a cartoon showing two men in a boat. Underneath the cartoon was the caption, "Tip the canoe and Tyler too."

Harrison was the first president to die in office. He had been

Clay's fine head of hair.

in his office for thirty days, working on new tariff laws, and probably overtaxed himself.

DANIEL WEBSTER.

A famous statesman and orator at this time was Daniel Webster. When he was on the Dartmouth College debating team, he spoke against the best-known debaters of the country, including the Devil, who represented Harvard. The trophies he won for debating are kept in the Dartmouth College Case. Although he was admitted to the bar when he was only nineteen, he never overindulged.

Webster was famous for using long words that other people could not spell, and therefore is said to have held his audiences spellbound. As he talked, his cousin Noah took these words down and eventually published them in a large volume called *Webster's Dictionary*.

———◆———

55

CHAPTER XX

THE WINNING OF TEXAS.

THE FRONTIER continued to move westward. Many adventurous persons, not wishing to be left behind, moved along with it. Some went by the Sante Fe, which at that time was only a trail, and had no diner. Some, who followed the inland waterways, used prairie schooners. There were many dangerous characters abroad, and not a few in our own country. Cardsharps and outcasts from places like Poker Flat were always ready to get up a game in a Canasta wagon.

KIT CARSON.

Kit Carson was one of the famous frontiersmen of his day. He was also a backwoodsman. For this reason he is said to have known the West backwoods and forewoods. As a young man, he was a scout; as a boy, he was a boy scout. The daring deeds of Kit Carson are in no way minimized in a book about them which was written by Kit Carson.

DAVY CROCKETT.

Another of the famed frontiersmen was Davy Crockett. He early proved his prowess with a rifle by shooting matches, which

Davy Crockett.

56

were too small a target for most of the sharpshooters of the day. His favorite costume was a coonskin cap and a buckskin jacket. It is assumed that he wore trousers of some sort, although they are never mentioned. After many exploits in Tennessee, he went on to Texas, which welcomed men of his caliber (.45). He wound up in the Alamo.

THE ALAMO.

Texas was then a part of Mexico because of Spain. Mexico had thrown off the Spanish yoke a few years earlier, but Texas was still wearing the Mexican yoke. Because this was before Theodore Roosevelt (see below), America was not yet an Imperialist Nation.

Americans living in Texas disagreed with the Mexicans who lived there; and Mexicans, and especially Mexican food,[1] disagreed with the Americans.

Finally the Americans declared that Texas was no longer a part of Mexico, and a small body of Americans moved into a landmark called the Alamo and waited to be outnumbered.[2] They were soon accommodated by a huge army of Mexican generals, who killed the defenders of the Alamo to the last man, whom they also killed.

The triumph of the Mexicans was short-lived, as also were many of the Mexican generals. If they expected the Americans to forget all about the Alamo, they were wrong. By saying "Remember the Alamo" over and over, especially just before going to sleep, the Americans were able to remember the name of the place for weeks and weeks. Later they remembered the Maine and after that Pearl Harbor.

SAM HOUSTON.

The leader of Texas's fight for independence was Sam Houston. He was in a class by himself, having gone to a small country school. When Texas became a republic, he was its first presi-

---

[1] Notably Mexican jumping beans, which refused to stay down.

[2] Being outnumbered is a requirement for going down in history, or even for going down.

dent, and when Texas joined the Union [1] he became a senator. In Washington, he was feared and respected by his fellow senators, possibly because he always carried a knife. They addressed him as "the distinguished Senator from Texas." He referred to them as "You-all."

WAR WITH MEXICO.

A dispute arose over the boundary between Texas and Mexico. The Americans thought that South of the Border was too far north, and the Mexicans did not like the way the Americans took the final *"e"* off the Rio Grande. There was a clash

General Infield Scott driving to Mexico City.

of arms. And then legs. War was on. Three of our finest leaders were the great generals Zachary Taylor, Old Rough, and Ready, who joined forces to defeat the Mexicans at Buenas Noches. General Infield Scott, who liked to fight up close, then drove all the way to Mexico City. This, considering the condition of Mexican roads, was such an impressive feat that the Mexicans were glad to sue for peace. The United States won the suit and was awarded California, Nevada, Utah, and a number of other states that were badly needed to fill up the map.

[1] Or, from the point of view of Texans, when the Union joined Texas.

CHAPTER XXI.

THE WINNING OF CALIFORNIA.

CALIFORNIA was discovered by John C. Frémont. This was thought unnecessary by the Mexicans and the Indians who were living there at the time, but they could not speak English and so did not count. On his way to California, Frémont followed the north fork of the Platte, which was just above the south fork. He endured terrible hardships, including the failure of many persons to put the accent in his name, even though he reminded them repeatedly. On one occasion his food supply ran so low that he was forced to eat his own horse, from which he first dismounted. Altogether he traveled six thousand miles, partly on horseback and partly on a full stomach.

Frémont discovering California.

THE GOLD RUSH.

More important than the discovery of California was the discovery of gold, a soft metal which nevertheless comes in for some hard use. Gold was discovered in a sawmill belonging to a Mr. Sutter. Since it interfered with the operation of the saw, it was removed as quickly as possible.

Thanks to clear atmospheric conditions, the cry, "Gold!

Gold!" was heard across the country. The Forty Niners, a group of forty-nine unkempt old men who chewed tobacco and never shaved, were among the first to arrive. Others were not far behind, including O. Henry, O. Susanna, and Mother Lode. They came by the thousands, and also by the Horn, which was several months slower. With them they brought picks, shovels, and a generous supply of stakes with which to stake claims. Because their wagons were so full of household goods, they carried their banjos on their knees.

Gold was mostly found in creek beds and was removed in bedpans. Since it was necessary to squat while at work, many of the miners were called squatters.

LIFE IN OLD CALIFORNIA.

Californians who were unsuccessful in finding gold went into other enterprises. Some went into business. Some went into professions. Almost everyone went into saloons. There were no lawyers, since people took the law into their own hands.

Because of lust for gold, morals reached a low point, known as the gold standard. No respectable woman would be seen in a music hall, and very few respectable women were seen anywhere, except young schoolteachers who had recently come from the East and still had a lot to learn. Card players, who

The Quick and the Dead.

played for high stakes and sometimes for money, had a nervous habit of shooting each other over trivial matters, such as almost invisible marks on cards or one or two extra aces in a deck. Persons who pulled their pistols out of their holsters first were known as the Quick; the others were the Dead.

———◆———

CHAPTER XXII.

THE WINNING OF OREGON.

OREGON was discovered when someone followed the Oregon Trail right out to the end.

Early settlers in Oregon were mostly fur traders looking for beaver hats. These they obtained by swapping sticks, or trading posts. One of the leading traders was John Jacob Astor, a wealthy New York hotel man who wished to take furs back to Lady Astor so that she could keep up with the Vanderbilts.

The journey over the Oregon Trail took several months. The plains were crossed in wagon trains or caravans, and the streams were crossed in Fords. At night the wagons were lined up around a hollow square. The women and children were put in the square, and the men, who were known as "square shooters," shot off Indians as they rode around and around on their horses. The Indians who had not been shot off, rode off. Crossing the desert was especially hazardous because of mirages, which were

Trading posts.

61

pools of water caused by thirst. The early travelers were slow to realize that the water in these pools was not good for drinking.

TROUBLE WITH THE BRITISH.

The British were in possession of most of Oregon and scornfully referred to the American fur traders as "furriners." The Americans offered to buy Oregon for $54.40, but the British considered this a disgracefully low figure, and wanted more latitude. This, however, was the Americans' last offer, and they said, "Fifty-four forty or fight." Rather than risk another war, the British let Oregon go for this price and withdrew across the Canadian border, taking their customs with them. Owing to American enterprise, the population doubled in a short time, which was the reason for cities like Walla Walla.

CHAPTER XXIII

THE MORMONS.

THE MORMONS are a group of people who became saints later than others and are thus known as Later-day Saints. Because their customs were different, they were forced to move from place to place. For settlers, this was an unsettling experience.

Bigamy Young.

62

But cheerfully, they pushed their handcarts over the mountains, thus becoming known as Good-humor Men.

They finally took over Utah and the Great Salt Lake, which no one else wanted. This was called the Mormon Conquest.

Their leader in the early days in Utah was Bigamy Young. When he arrived in Salt Lake City he said to his followers, "This is the place," although he had never been there before. It was uncanny.

Under Young's leadership, the Mormons prospered. They were industrious, thrifty folk, and good at arithmetic and keeping accounts, as for instance the number of their cattle, sheep, and wives. They multiplied rapidly. The women who objected to plural marriages were considered singular.

The Mormons are credited with having made the desert bloom, which it continues to do each spring.

———◆———

CHAPTER XXIV.

FOUR PRESIDENTS.

ALL this while there were several presidents, one at a time. Being small men, they stood on platforms to make themselves look bigger. These were built by party hacks, who made use of such devices as old saws and the rank and file. In order to be elected it was necessary to make campaign promises, which had to be kept for the duration of the campaign. Upon election, it was the custom to swear oaths. These were listened to without flinching by the Chief Justice of the Supreme Court, who was considered a good judge of such things.

JOHN TYLER.

As we have seen, John Tyler was in the tippy canoe with Harrison, and paddled to office up the Potomac. He was the first vice-president to become president through the death of a president, which was a good thing for him but a bad thing for Harrison.

63

Although he was elected to office as a Wig, the Wigs later disowned him because he insisted on wearing his own hair. For a time he was a man without a party, which annoyed his wife, who loved to entertain.

It was during Tyler's presidency that China opened its doors to American traders, with the proviso that they take off their shoes before coming inside. This led to friendly relations with the Chinese, who came to the United States in large numbers to open laundries and restaurants and to teach young Americans to play "Chopsticks" on the piano.

JAMES K. POLK.

Polk was the first president to enter the race as a dark horse. Only after he had won the race and was installed in the White House was it discovered that he was actually a horse of another color. He was forgiven for this deception, but never became popular.[1]

Much trouble was caused during Polk's term by the Free Soilers, a group of unreasonable men who wanted to get everything dirty and refused to pay their laundry bills. On the other hand, progress was made by the invention of the Rotary printing press. This went around and around and preceded by several years the next development in this field, the Kiwanis.

ZACHARY TAYLOR.

Owing to his defeat of the Mexicans at Buenas Noches, General Taylor became a national hero. It turned out to be only a step from Buenas Noches to the presidency, and the General took this in his stride.

General Taylor is remembered as the only president who ever rode a horse up the steps of the Capitol. Eminent historians agree that he was probably the only president who ever wanted to. At any rate, it is fortunate for the custodians of the building that this bad precedent has not been followed.

[1] He redeemed himself slightly by introducing the folk dance that bears his name, the Polka.

One of the most important pieces of legislation during Taylor's term was the Omnibus Bill, introduced by Henry Clay. This would have provided omnibuses in California, Utah, New Mexico, and Texas, which were large territories and badly in need of transportation. Taylor opposed the Omnibus Bill, however, because he thought it would mean the end of the horse. He was not sure which end, but he had always been a horse lover.[1]

It was also while Taylor was president that the Department of the Inferior was created to improve conditions among the underprivileged third of the nation.

After a brief period in office, Zachary Taylor died with his boots on, but in bed.

MILLARD FILLMORE.

Millard Fillmore inherited the presidency from Zachary Taylor. This was discovered when Taylor's will was read.

Commodore Perry
opens up Japan.

Fillmore achieved a certain amount of distinction by the Compromise of 1850, in which he gave away a little to the North and a little to the South. The possessor of a keen his-

[1]Cf. Taylor's classical expression, "Equus vincit omnibus."

torical sense, Fillmore was saving the Civil War for Lincoln, who could handle it.

A significant development at this time was Commodore Perry's expedition to open up Japan so that Americans could see what was inside.[1] They were startled to discover that it was teeming with Japanese, who enjoyed a high birth rate.

Perry's opening of Japan caused many Japanese to come out where they could see the rising sun. As a result of this, Japan soon developed modern methods. (See Pearl Harbor, below.)

[1] This was later viewed with alarm by a funereal-looking newspaperman named William Randolph Hearse. He wrote so much about the Yellow Peril that his journalism took its distinctive coloration from the subject.

THIRD TEST.

Some of these statements are either true or false. Indicate which ones are neither.

1. Napoleon sold Louisiana because he knew he could not compete with Huey Long.

2. If the British owned Oregon today, and it were worth $54.40, what would they receive for it, net? (Hint: Convert the price into sterling at $2.80 to the pound, then deduct British income tax at the rate of 9 shillings 6 pence to the pound, and you'll find it a lot easier to move on to the next question.)

3. You can reach the high notes in "The Star-Spangled Banner" by standing on tiptoe.

4. Dolly Madison was stronger than Dolly Varden.

5. The Morse code is so profane that it is necessary to resort to dashes.

6. Housewives in early California were constantly annoyed by the gold dust.

7. No one ever traveled east on the Oregon Trail because it was longer that way.

8. The Alamo is easier to remember than Polk, Tyler, or Fillmore.

CHAPTER XXV.

THE SLAVERY QUESTION.

THE QUESTION that was most often asked at this time was the slavery question. It was hardly ever answered. John C. Calhoun, a champion of the Southern cause, asked the question more often than anyone else in the South. William Lloyd Garrison, a champion of the Northern cause, out-asked everyone in the North. Calhoun thought slavery was a good thing. Garrison, on the other hand, was an Abolitionist. He wanted to do away with slaves—a bloodthirsty proposal that made the kindly Southern plantation owners shudder.

H. B. STOWE.

The slavery question would probably have remained a question had it not been for Harriet Beechnut Stowe, a self-reliant, determined woman who lived with her Uncle Tom in a humble cabin. At first she was only mildly against slavery, and called it a Little Evil, but later she changed her mind because of an unpleasant experience with a planter named Slimy Legree, who pursued her across the ice while she was carrying Topsy. Despite her condition, she managed to get away by jumping from one piece of ice to another faster than her pursuer.[1] This left her terribly cold toward Legree and all he stood for. As a result, she wrote a famous book praising the Negro, called *Black Beauty*, that incited people in the North to acts of violence, including setting fire to slave-owners' barns.

The slavery question then became a Burning Issue.

THE UNDERGROUND RAILROAD.

Slaves were sold in the South by being auctioned off. Entire city squares, called auction blocks, were devoted to these sales. Buyers often felt slaves' muscles to see whether they would be good workers. They also looked at their teeth, in case they were to be used for plowing.

[1] While she was slowed down by Topsy, Legree was slightly tipsy.

As if they were their own children.

Slaves were treated by many Southerners as if they were their own children, and yet some of them ungratefully ran away. For this purpose the slaves cleverly built an underground railway all the way to Canada. Trains (including the extra-fare *Dixie Flyer*) left almost daily from tracks on the lower level called the Deep South. Slaves usually bought a one-way ticket.

THE DREAD SCOTT DECISION.

The Dread Scott Decision was one that frightened everybody. It decided that a slave who lived in a free state was free to be a slave, but would be happier if he lived in a slave state where slavery was appreciated. This was not only frightening but confusing. Even the Supreme Court was forced to admit it had no jurisdiction, which meant that it was unable to figure it out. As might be imagined, everyone was in a state.

JOHN BROWN.

John Brown was a brave but foolhardy man (*i.e.*, a Fanatic) who tried to seize arms from Northerners and give them to slaves. The Northerners were willing to give him a hand, but thought this was going too far. So they hanged poor John Brown and left his body on Harper's Ferry, where it lay moldering until the passengers complained.

War was in the air.

CHAPTER XXVI.

PRESIDENTS PIERCE AND BUCHANAN.

MANY PERSONS have difficulty remembering what President Franklin Pierce is best remembered for, and he is therefore probably best forgotten.

President James Buchanan is known as The Only President Who Never Married, and thus has become extremely useful in quizzes and crossword puzzles. An important event of his administration was the establishment of the pony express, which made it possible to ship ponies anywhere in the United States as long as they were securely wrapped.

The Pony Express.

The Civil War was ready to begin during Buchanan's term, but everyone thought it better to wait until Lincoln so that it could begin and end under the same president.

CHAPTER XXVII.

ABRAHAM LINCOLN.

ABRAHAM LINCOLN was the Man of the Hour. In those days this was almost as important as being Man of the Year or Book of the Month

During his youth he lived in several different log cabins, a style of architecture favored by his father. He was born in only two of them, the Original and the Reconstructed.

Young Abe loved to read. Since he had no library card, he had difficulty borrowing books and obtaining advice about what to read. On one occasion he walked many miles to get Blackstone's commentaries. Blackstone apparently suggested the Bible, from which Lincoln copied out favorite passages with a piece of charcoal on a shingle and thus evolved a simple, if rather wooden, style. Lincoln always read lying on his stomach in front of an open fireplace. Thus he developed an insatiable curiosity and a sacroiliac condition.

Lincoln became known as Honest Abe when he was working as a clerk in a store. Once he walked three miles to return six cents to a woman. When he told the woman he had overcharged her, she was surprised and said, "Honest, Abe?" The name followed him through life, and often caught up with him.

Renowned for his feats of strength, Lincoln was of great use to the early railroads. A champion rail-splitter, he was able to split a rail with one blow of his ax, thus making two tracks out of it.[1]

Lincoln had one term in Congress and then ran for the Senate because, as he said in a famous speech, "The House is divided against itself and cannot stand." He wanted to get out before the roof caved in.

As president, Lincoln was always traveling about the country to meet people and to sign commissions which were kept in attics until the value of Lincoln's signature went up. It was difficult to get his mail to him because of his many addresses, such as the First Inaugural, the Second Inaugural, and the Gettysburg. This latter he jotted down on the back of an envelope instead of the front, but it came through all right.[2]

Lincoln is now popularly known for being "heads" when one is matching pennies.

[1] Lincoln's ability as a rail-splitter later proved useful in politics. Most of his opponents, considerably weaker men, were hair-splitters.

[2] The Post Office Department was then at the peak of its efficiency.

CHAPTER XXVIII.

THE CIVIL WAR.

WAR finally broke out when some of the Southern states decided to secede. It was their firm belief that nothing succeeds like secession. They named Jeff Davis their president and raised their own flag, it being possible to raise almost anything in the fertile soil of the South.

Lincoln, who was a kindly man, insisted that if there had to be a war it should at least be fought as decently as possible. It was therefore spoken of as the Civil War. It was fought between the boys in blue (who wore Union suits) and the boys in gray, although most of the boys were old enough to have whiskers and did.

The battle cries of the two forces were "On to Washington" and "On to Richmond." Each was after the other's capital, and the North, being industrial, had more capital than the South. If the North had permitted the South to take Washington and the South had permitted the North to take Richmond, the war might have been won by both sides and everyone would have been happy. Apparently the opposing generals did not take this under serious consideration.

The Civil War.

U. S. Grant and friends.

GRANT AND LEE.

The greatest general of the North was U. S. Grant, who is not to be confused with U. S. Mail or U. S. Steel. In a picture of the Northern generals, all of whom have identical untidy black whiskers, he is usually the one in the center with his coat unbuttoned. Grant was the victim of repeated attacks. After one of these he took Vicksburg, which had a tonic effect.

The Southern leader was Robert E. Lee, who had better manners but fewer soldiers than Grant. Promotion was slow in his army, and most of his high-ranking officers never became more than Lee's lieutenants. To distinguish him when he is in a picture with Grant, Lee is the one with the white whiskers sitting on Traveller, who was a horse. After the war, Lee bought a half interest in Washington and Lee University in nearby Virginia.

OTHER GENERALS.

Two of the leading generals of the North were Sheridan and Sherman. Sheridan is known for his famous Ride and Sherman for his famous March, which is noteworthy because it lasted well into December. Some of Sherman's exploits are almost unbelievable. We are told that he cut a path sixty miles wide through the South, although this was surely wider than neces-

73

sary. He also sacked Atlanta, after which he carried it all the way to the sea.

Lee's most able general (or lieutenant) was Stonewall Jackson. When Jackson died, it is said that Lee lost his right arm, which made it difficult for him to hold the reins.

Most of the other generals were named Johnston.

FAMOUS BATTLES.

The first great battle of the Civil War was fought in a cow pasture and was known as Bull Run. The battle was such a success that it was repeated by popular request.

The other important battles were all fought at some burg or other, such as Petersburg, Fredericksburg, Gettysburg, and Williamsburg. Williamsburg was so badly damaged that it had to be restored.[1] The most decisive of these battles was Gettysburg, where the Confederates, who by this time were low on ammunition, swept up the hill with sharpened stakes in what was called Pickets Charge.

At sea, meanwhile, there was a famous engagement between two "ironclads," the *Christian Science Monitor* and the *Merrimac*. Since neither could sink the other, and they could not wait to see which one would rust first, they agreed to call it a draw.

SURRENDER.

The end came in a memorable action at Appomattox Court House, where Grant, who was more experienced at the bar, won a clear-cut decision. This brought tears to the eyes of Lee's soldiers, and they were overcome. Lee then gave his sword to Grant, but Grant gave it back to him, since he already had one. Jefferson Davis joined the ranks of the unemployed.

---

[1] The Rockefellers paid for this, even though they had not been responsible for the damage.

MID-TERM PROJECTS (OPTIONAL).

1. Read one other book about the Civil War. This will make you a specialist.

2. Split a rail in remembrance of Abe Lincoln. If this is too difficult, lie on the floor in front of an open fireplace. If you have no fireplace and happen to work behind a cash register, shortchange your next customer and then follow him for six miles through a raging blizzard to see that he gets what's coming to him.

3. Draw detailed maps of the following:

    (*a*) Sheridan's Ride

    (*b*) Lee's Surrender

    (*c*) Grant's Tomb

4. Prepare a thirty-minute talk on the Siege of Richmond. Then find someone who will listen to it.

5. Visit the chapel at Washington and Lee University and look at the mounted skeleton of Traveller. If you were a college, couldn't you think of a more appropriate way to dispose of a dead horse?

CHAPTER XXIX.

RECONSTRUCTION.

AFTER the Civil War, the South was swept by a wave of carpet-beggars who went from door to door begging carpets from the poor Southerners, many of whom did not even have floors. They were told to come back after the Reconstruction.

Carpetbeggers and Ku Klux Klan.

The carpetbeggars were especially disliked by the Ku Klux Klan, a group of Southerners who had nothing to wear but sheets with holes in them [1] and always looked as if they had just come from a Halloween party. It was these Klux who introduced phonetic spelling and gave us such words as Kleenex, Krispies, and Krazy Kat.

PRESIDENTS JOHNSON AND GRANT.

Reconstruction was begun by President Johnson and completed by President Grant, who financed it by selling copies of his two-volume *Memoirs* to everyone in America.

MONEY TROUBLES.

During Grant's administration a good deal of trouble was caused by money, which people had previously considered

[1] Thus they became known as "poor whites."

man's best friend. Outstanding troubles were the following:

1. *Black Friday.* This was due to Jay Gould, who wanted to buy up every bit of money and make the United States go on the Gould standard. He was assisted in this nefarious plan by an ex-slave called Black Friday, who was always leaving footprints in unexpected places. It was because of Friday that Gould was finally tracked down.

2. *Specie Payments.* The origin of the Specie is attributed to Darwin. It is often called Hard Money, as opposed to Easy Money. In order to make hard money easier, bits of specie were buried in government vaults until they mildewed and became greenbacks.

3. *Silver Act.* This was one of Grant's unwisest acts. It was put over by the hard-money people, who considered gold too soft and thought it should be made harder by adding bits of silver.[1]

WHISKY RING.

One of the things that caused Grant's cabinet a great deal of trouble was the way a whisky glass, when set down on it, would leave a ring. Although Grant tried his best to cover it with whitewash, the Whisky Ring still showed through. This finally forced Grant to leave the White House in disgrace.

———◆———

CHAPTER XXX.

THE WILD WEST.

WHILE the rest of the country was being reconstructed, the West was still being constructed for the first time, and there was a great deal of wild life everywhere, especially in the towns. Men were men and women were women, and this simple ar-

[1] The only good that came of this was the popular song, "Silver Threads Among the Gold."

rangement proved quite satisfactory. Men who were in business together called each other "podner."

Life was hard in the Great Plains region. On the one hand there were the badmen, or Desperate Characters, like the James brothers, William and Henry. They held up stagecoaches, thus making them late, and withdrew other people's money from banks. On the other hand there were the Indians, like Geronimo and Sitting Bull, stubborn chieftains who claimed the Indians were there first and refused to budge.

BUFFALO BILL AND OTHERS.

Fortunately there were half a dozen crack shots,[1] known as the Six Shooters, on the side of law and order. One of these

*General Custer
(right)
vs. Crazy Quilt.*

was Wild Bill Hiccup, a man of few words, such as "Reach" and "Now git." He is said never to have killed a man except in self-defense, but he was defending himself almost constantly. Another was Buffalo Bill, a sharpshooter who had poison ivy on his hands and thus was bothered by an itching

[1] Able to shoot through narrow cracks and knotholes. To be distinguished from crackpots.

trigger finger. In his later years Buffalo Bill went into the circus business and shot it out with Annie Oakley.

CUSTER'S LAST STAND.

The badmen were usually defeated by the goodmen and the redmen by the whitemen, but occasionally there was a temporary setback. This was permanent in the case of Custer, who bravely stood up in plain sight and fought against all sorts of odds, including an Indian named Crazy Quilt. His last stand was at a place of uncertain size called Little Big Horn.

Without overlapping.

THE HOMESTEAD LAW.

To induce people to leave the East and face the hazards of life in states like Oklahoma, the government passed the Homestead Law. This gave everyone free land, provided he would guarantee to stay alive on it a certain length of time.[1] The Homesteaders lined up in their covered wagons and buggies at the state boundary and at a given signal were off on a race for choice lands. The best land seemed to be on top of a high mountain called Pikes Peak (or Bust), which rapidly became overpopulated. Those who could find no room there settled in

[1] See Edgar Guest's "It takes a heap o' livin' on to make a house a homestead."

Oklahoma and worked diligently to turn its rich land into the Dust Bowl.[1]

TRANSCONTINENTAL RAILROAD.

A great stride was taken in the development of the West when a railroad was finally built all the way across the country. This railroad was begun at both ends and came together, without overlapping, somewhere in Utah. To celebrate this instance of making ends meet, the two parts were fastened together with a gold spike, and the wilderness was no longer trackless.

[1] Oklahoma's answer to California's Rose Bowl.

CHAPTER XXXI.

FROM HAYES TO HARRISON.

THE PRESIDENTS in this period are difficult to tell apart, even though their parents gave them first names like Rutherford, Chester, and Grover to make it easier. To add to the confusion, Grover Cleveland was elected twice, with one president in between, which was constitutional but highly irregular.

With one president in between.

Another thing that makes the presidents at this time hard to distinguish is that they were not very distinguished; so if some of them get mislaid here, it is a safe assumption that they will never be missed.

GROVER CLEVELAND.

As a politician, Cleveland made his name in Buffalo. Unlike Chester A. Arthur, who became honest after becoming president, Cleveland started earlier. When he ran for governor of New York, he said he was an "unowned candidate." This proved quite upsetting to the members of Tammany Hall, who thought he said he was an "unknown candidate," which would have been all right.

Cleveland was elected president as a Democrat with the help of the Mugwumps, a group of uncertain Republicans who, as we have often been told, sat with their mugs on one side of the fence and their wumps on the other. In some cases it was hard to tell which was which.

Mugwumps.

As soon as he became president, Cleveland instituted a number of reforms, the first of which was to remove Republicans from office. This was a distinct surprise to them, because for years they had thought, as they put it, that "public office is a Republican trust."

The Republicans still caused trouble, however, because they had won most of the seats in Congress and the Democrats were forced to stand.

BENJAMIN HARRISON.

Harrison is best remembered because he is the president who was sandwiched in between Cleveland's first term and second term. With Cleveland both over and under him in the list of presidents, his place in history is secure and he is not likely to move an inch.[1]

[1] The reader may be interested to know that President Benjamin Harrison was the grandson of President William Henry Harrison. And then again he may not.

CHAPTER XXXII.

THE AGE OF INDUSTRY.

NEW FACTORIES began springing up everywhere. Articles that had formerly been made by hand were now made by machines, although a few continued to be handmade, with irregularities and imperfections, for the lucky persons who could afford them. In addition to factories, there were numerous sweatshops. These were rooms in overheated homes, where women and small children worked long hours so that the man of the house could maintain his credit at the corner saloon. Sometimes the golden-haired daughter would go to the saloon and beg her dear father to come home with her, which he often would do in order to beat up his family. This was called Intemperance and was frowned on.

Intemperance.

IMMIGRATION.

People came from all over the world to work in American factories, standing in long assembly lines to seek employment. When they left their home country, they were called "emigrants," but this was Anglicized to "immigrants" when they reached the Land of Opportunity, as the United States was called on maps printed in Europe.

Before being permitted to work in American factories, immigrants had their foreign customs removed by customs officials and were thoroughly cleaned in what was called a melting pot. Those who could stand the intense heat were considered ready for the sweatshops.

LABOR UNREST.

In the early days [1] a laborer sometimes worked twelve or fourteen hours. He had little time for sleep, and this unfortunate situation became known as Labor Unrest. Workingmen decided to strike (a blow for freedom) and thus, unwittingly, started the Industrial Revolution.

In order to help the laborers strike better, or at least to strike the right people, Samuel Gompers organized the American Federation of Labor. Members of the AFL carried cards and thus were always able to get up a game when not working.[2]

The greatest contribution made by labor was the ingenious reform of the calendar, resulting in the eight-hour day and the five-day week.

CHAPTER XXXIII.

CAPTAINS OF INDUSTRY.

THIS was a period of great opportunities for enterprising young men. Most of the factories were one-story buildings, so it was easy to get in on the ground floor. As soon as additional stories were built, those who had started at the bottom worked their way up.

CORNELIUS VANDERBILT.

Vanderbilt made his money in ships. Thus, while others became captains of industry, he became a commodore. He also

---

[1] The early days were so called because the workingman had to get up at five o'clock.

[2] They also carried signs, reading "Unfair," to keep from getting struck themselves.

bought up railroads so that he could always be sure of getting a lower berth. His control of carts and cartels gave him a virtual monotony of transportation. One of his favorite expressions, which endeared him to everyone, was "The public be damned."

ANDREW CARNEGIE.

Carnegie made his money in steel. Although he was a mild, soft-spoken man, his steel had quite a temper. Most of it was made in open hearths, then fashionable in the better homes of Pittsburgh. Thanks largely to Carnegie's efforts, steel rapidly came to replace wood in almost everything but trees.

In a short while Carnegie, who had come to this country as a poor boy from Scotland, amassed such wealth that he was loved by everyone. He was especially popular because of his determination to give away all his money before he died.[1] In order to succeed in this, he was forced to retire early, since he was making money faster than he could give it away. He is best remembered for having given away libraries, with his name on them, in which everyone was asked to be quiet out of respect for the donor. Carnegie was so well known for his philanthropy that he became an Institution.

JOHN D. ROCKEFELLER.

Rockefeller made his money in oil, which he discovered at the bottom of wells. Oil was crude in those days, but so was Rockefeller. Now both are considered quite refined.

Almost everyone called Rockefeller "John D." A few called him something else, but not to his face. He was admired for his skill in a game called Monopoly, which was an effective way of eliminating competitors and establishing a single standard, such as Standard Oil.

Rockefeller's huge fortune seemed even larger than it was because he kept it in dimes.

[1] See his book on giving away money, *How to Win Friends and Influence People.*

Rockefeller's dimes.

J. P. MORGAN.

Morgan, who was a direct sort of person, made his money in money. He lived in an airy mansion, full of bank drafts, called the House of Morgan. One of the gayest persons in the house was Helen Morgan, who sat on top of the piano when she sang.

An ingenious invention of Morgan's was a means of floating government loans which made it possible to send large sums of money across the Atlantic without using ships. He became immensely wealthy because of his financial interests, most of which were around eight or ten per cent. This Morgan is usually spoken of as "J.P." to distinguish him from Henry Morgan, the pirate.

HENRY FORD.

Henry Ford manufactured one of the early automobiles, known as the Model T. This led to such modern conveniences as traffic signals, parking meters, back-seat drivers, and carbon monoxide. In time it came to replace the horse for almost all purposes except horse racing and horsemeat. An idealist and a dreamer, this great inventor dreamed of two cars in every garage—both of them Fords. Henry Ford was fond of saying, "History is bunk." Historians, in turn, called Henry Ford "a damned old crankshaft."

CHAPTER XXXIV.

NEW INVENTIONS.

INVENTIONS were necessary at this time so that factories would have something to manufacture. Before an invention could be invented, however, four things were required:

1. Necessity, the mother of inventions.
2. An inventor, the father of inventions.
3. A basement, back room, or small shed, where the birth of the invention could take place.
4. A patent, or birth certificate.[1]

THE ELECTRIC LIGHT.

The man who was first with almost all the new inventions was Thomas ("Alpha") Edison. He is best remembered for having been thrown off a train for inventing things in the baggage car when he should have been selling newspapers. He lit on his head and became so deaf that he was unable to hear discouraging remarks and soon became successful.

Since Edison suffered from insomnia, he invented the electric light, so that he could read at night. He had to sweat it out, and this led him to make his famous remark: "Genius is about 2 per cent inspiration and 98 per cent perspiration."

THE TELEPHONE.

The telephone was invented by Alexander Graham Bell, after whom the telephone bell is named. He was also responsible for the telephone exchange, where old phones could be traded in for French models. Other outgrowths of the telephone include the telephone booth, in which one has the choice of light or air, and the telephone book, a large volume that permits almost everyone to see his name in print.

The telephone revolutionized American life and introduced such improvements as the party line, the wrong number, the busy signal, and the long distance.

[1] Important patents included patent leather and patent medicine.

THE RADIO.

We are indebted for the radio to an Italian by the name of Macaroni. An inconspicuous person, he was not recognized in his native land and was forced to make his career in England and the United States.

The radio is also called the wireless, especially in England. This is because, although there are a great many wires in it, there are less than there might be. The great improvement of the radio over the telephone is that it may be turned off without offending the speaker.

THE AIRPLANE.

The airplane was invented by the Wright brothers and a girl friend named Kitty Hawk. They were at first thought crazy, which assured them of ultimate success. The airplane revolutionized transportation, making it possible to cross the United States in a few hours and crash almost anywhere.

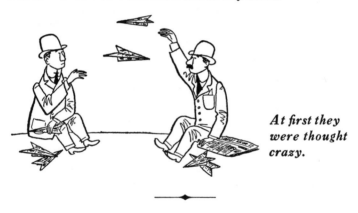

At first they were thought crazy.

CHAPTER XXXV.

PRESIDENT McKINLEY.

THE ELECTION of 1896 was one of the most stirring in American history. Sediment ran high. McKinley ran on the Republican

The Vested Interests.

ticket and Bryan, who had the wind but not the legs, ran on the Democratic ticket. One of the important issues in the election was gold versus silver. Bryan was for silver, and talked about it so much that he was said to have a silver tongue.

On the other hand, McKinley was for gold, which gained him the backing of a group of well-dressed financiers known as the Vested Interests. He conducted a front-porch campaign (Bryan meanwhile skulking around in the back), and was assisted by a bossy woman always referred to simply as Hannah. The election was finally won by McKinley, but Bryan was not discouraged. He ran in several more presidential races until Clarence Darrow finally made a monkey out of him in Tennessee.

THE BOXER REBELLION.

One of the disturbing events of McKinley's administration was the Boxer Rebellion. This occurred when Chinese prize fighters thought they were being treated unfairly by foreign referees, such as an Irishman by the name of Hoyle, whom everything was always according to, and that notorious rake, the Marquis of Queensberry. After a good deal of unpleasantness, the matter was settled amicably by giving the boxers scholarships to study the rules of the ring at American universities.

———◆———

CHAPTER XXXVI.

THE SPANISH-AMERICAN WAR.

THE SPANISH-AMERICAN WAR, which occurred at the turn of the century,[1] was caused by Cuba. The United States wanted Cuba free [2] but Spain would not even sell it. It was thought that if Cuba could throw off the Spanish yoke, which increased the overhead, Havana tobacco would be less expensive. And it was widely believed that what this country needed was a good five-cent cigar.

So much to remember.

Conditions became tense when the battleship *Maine,* which was in Havana Harbor, exploded and sank to the bottom. Americans resented this, because they recalled the old saying. "As the *Maine* goes, so goes the nation." All over the country, citi-

[1] The turn of the century encompasses the period from 1875 to 1925. The nineteenth century turned very slowly.

[2] Whence the name of the popular drink of that day, the *Cuba Libre.*

zens who had been busy remembering the Alamo were now asked to remember the *Maine*. With so much to remember, nerves were on edge and war was inevitable.

The first blow was struck in Manila Bay, where the American fleet was stationed to protect our interest in Manila envelopes and other indispensable commodities. The fleet was under the command of Commodore Dewey, who cleverly sailed up behind the Spanish ships and for this exploit was made a rear admiral. A considerate commander, his immortal words on this occasion were, "You may fire when ready, Gridley." Unfortunately for the Spanish fleet, Gridley was ready.

On land, meanwhile, the Americans won a great victory when Colonel Roosevelt's Rough Riders, a band of cavalrymen who were hard on their clothes and easy on their horses, crawled up San Wan Hill on their stomachs. Their mounts were therefore fresh when they reached the top, and they were able to dash down again in fine style.

The United States did not get Cuba out of the Spanish-American War, but it got Puerto Rico, the Philippines, Guam, Typhoid, and Malaria. These were considered sufficient to make her a world power and only one or two possessions short of imperialistic.

FOURTH TEST.

1. How would you confuse
   (*a*) Black Friday and Blue Monday?
   (*b*) The James brothers?
2. Discuss the following terms:
   (*a*) Greenbacks
   (*b*) Whitewash
   (*c*) Blackmail
3. How many pear-shaped vowels do you find in the word "Mugwump"? Do you still like pears?
4. Complete the quotation, "Where men were men and women were ——."
5. Do you think any of the present-day wonder drugs would have helped Buffalo Bill's itching trigger finger?
6. Estimate the relative temperature of
   (*a*) Sweatshops
   (*b*) Turkish baths
7. Why on earth did Rockefeller want so much money?
8. List five situations in which it would have been better if the electric light had not been invented.

CHAPTER XXXVII.

THEODORE ROOSEVELT.

THEODORE ROOSEVELT was one of our best-known presidents, being known as T. R., Teddy, and Not Franklin. He was an Oyster Bay Roosevelt, which is one of the two principal varieties.

As a boy, Roosevelt was weak and sickly, but he built himself up by boxing and taking exercises with dumbbells in a gymnasium. Gradually he became more and more robust, despite several years at Harvard. He liked the out-of-doors, and bought a large amount of it on a ranch in North Dakota, the acquisition of which he modestly described as "The Winning of the West."

Roosevelt grew so muscular that the politicians deemed it wise to put him on a shelf in the vice-presidency, where they thought he would be safe, not knowing that McKinley was so close to being shot.

When Roosevelt got down from the shelf and moved into the White House, the United States was at peace. The former Rough Rider found this intolerably dull and decided to make war on someone. The British, Japanese, Germans, Canadians, Russians, and Venezuelans were all considered. In a final act of desperation, Roosevelt sent the American fleet around the world

T. R. looks for a war.

looking for a suitable enemy. Unable to find one, he was forced to accept the Nobel Peace Prize as a consolation.

Roosevelt was known as a man of unquenchable energy. He paid little attention to rank, money, and social position, perhaps because he had so much of all three. He was deeply interested in nature, which he tried to conserve. He did this by collecting such natural resources as butterflies and birds, which he thought were being wasted. At the same time he was violently opposed to Big Business, then busily engaged in collecting money, Trusts, and other unnatural things. As might be expected, Roosevelt was greatly annoyed when the Trusts sneeringly referred to him as "Buster."

At the conclusion of his term, Roosevelt went West to find his successor and picked a hearty, pioneer type named William Howard Taft. This done, he went off to Darkest Africa where, despite the poor light, he bagged many magnificent specimens and brought them home for zoos and museums. One specimen of which he was especially proud was the bull moose, which he captured by speaking softly and then hitting it on the head with a big stick.

THE MUCKRAKERS.

The Muckrakers were exceedingly fond of muck, which they raked up into large piles and gazed at admiringly.

One of the leading muckrakers was Upton Sinclair, who raked up a huge pile in South Chicago. While raking, Sinclair could not help noticing the terrible conditions in the nearby stockyards, where innocent cattle were being driven to slaughter instead of being coaxed. He wrote a book about this called *The Jungle*, which was read by President Roosevelt, who thought it was about Africa. Roosevelt was indignant when he read about the treatment being given these poor animals, and introduced a law providing that they should be killed only by sportsmen wearing pith helmets.

A lady muckraker named Carrie Nation was responsible for legislation that required printing the alcoholic content on the label so that sick people would know whether they were getting

Sportsman wearing
pith helmet.

enough alcohol to do them any good. Soon afterwards came
the Poor Food and Drug Act. This made it mandatory for
manufacturers to tell whether their product was a poor food or
a drug so that the consumer would know whether to keep it in
the kitchen or in the bathroom.

THE PANAMA CANAL.

The Panama Canal was built to make it possible for the
Atlantic and Pacific Oceans to come together without having
to go clear around South America. Digging was begun under
Roosevelt (but, luckily, not directly under him), and was finished several presidents later. For a time work was delayed by
mosquitoes, which the workmen were kept busy slapping with
their shovels. Science came to the rescue when the bothersome
insects were injected with yellow fever and died like flies.

————◆————

CHAPTER XXXVIII.

TAFT.

THE NEXT president is chiefly remembered for his size. He was
about as big around as two ordinary men, and was fortunately

named both William and Howard. His great hunger (and wealth) led him to demand steaks for breakfast.[1] Since he was too large for most chairs, he spent most of his life on the bench. Roosevelt leaned heavily on him when he was in his cabinet, but Taft was very good-natured about it.

Fortunately named both William and Howard.

DOLLAR DIPLOMACY.

Because of his long years on the bench, Taft was no longer a young man when he finally got into the game. Once in, however, he made his weight felt. His policy of dollar diplomacy, *i.e.*, hiring dollar-a-year men, was considered a master stroke of economy.

THE PROGRESSIVES.

When Taft ran for reelection, the Republican Party was unable to get anywhere. It had been bolted by the Progressives,[2] under a pugnacious chap with a fine head of hair named "Fighting Bob" La Follicle.

Taft tried to keep in the middle of the road and succeeded. He was run over by the Democratic machine.

[1] Thus becoming widely known as the Autocrat of the Breakfast Table.
[2] Laborers very handy with a wrench.

CHAPTER XXXIX.

WILSON.

WOODROW WILSON is the president who is usually pictured sitting in the back of an open car with a top hat and an overcoat on. The man sitting next to him is the head of some European government who also wears a top hat and would wear an overcoat if he had one. A Princeton man, Wilson was known as The Scholar President, and even after he got to the White House he was always in a brown study.

FINANCIAL REFORM.

Money continued to be badly distributed, and the demand was greater than even the counterfeiters could satisfy. Conditions were somewhat improved by establishment of the following:

1. *Federal Reserve System.* This involved the printing of Federal notes, which the government generously sent to banks all over the country to save them the expense of printing their own.

2. *Income Tax.* The income tax came into being with passage of the Underwood Act (sometimes referred to as the Underhand Act). People were put into tax brackets where they were held securely until they gave up. Most of them gave up plenty.[1]

MEXICAN BORDER WAR.

An obscure little war took place at this time with Mexico. As a matter of fact it only bordered on war, whence it derived its name. It was caused when a fat fellow named Pauncho Villa and his followers, known as the Four Horsemen of Acapulco, made daring raids into United States territory and breathed garlic into the faces of the terrified citizenry. President Wilson sent General Pershing (familiarly known as Blackjack because of his fondness for licorice chewing gum) down to capture

[1] Other taxes included sails taxes, aimed principally at yachtsmen, and hidden taxes, which were ashamed to come out in the open.

Villa. But Villa eluded his pursuers by hiding behind mesquite, mesquitoes, mustachios, and other features of the rugged Mexican terrain. All the Americans got out of the war was calluses, which the infantry and cavalry got in different places.

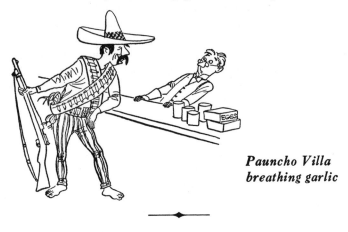

*Pauncho Villa
breathing garlic*

CHAPTER XL

WORLD WAR I.

WORLD WAR I was fought to make the world safe for the Democrats. There are different theories regarding its cause.[1] It is variously attributed to:

1. The fact that Germany wanted a place in the sun and was determined to take the French Riviera.

2. The Balkan powder keg, which was set off by a guy named Guy Fawkes who mistook the lower part of Europe for the lower house of Parliament.

3. The mistaken belief of Kaiser Wilhelm that the English would not fight against him because he was related to Queen Victoria.

4. A serious shortage of paper, which made a mere scrap of it worth fighting for.

[1] Any three of these constitute the Triple Intent.

The United States at first kept out of the war. President Wilson wrote numerous notes to the Kaiser, asking him to stop fighting. The Kaiser either ignored them or boorishly replied in German, which he thought Wilson could not read. Moreover he played Havoc (a German game) with American shipping, even though he soon ran through his first-string submarines and was down to his U-boats.

Finally Wilson, who had turned a deaf ear to those who wanted war, turned his good ear. He was shocked at what he heard.

THE WESTERN FRONT.

The AEF, later referred to as the American Legion, was sent to a part of France known as the Western Front or Over There. The first soldiers were enthusiastically greeted by Lafayette, the Mademoiselle from Armentières, and other French dignitaries, who kissed them on both cheeks. After a terrifying taxicab ride from Paris, they reached the trenches, where they soon acquired trench mouth, trench foot, and other soldierly habits that qualified them for membership in the Veterans of Foreign Wars.

The Americans fought bravely, frequently going over the top and over the hill and running into Germans who said

*Other
soldierly
habits.*

99

"Kamerad" or "Don't you remember me? We met in a beer garden in St. Louis." The hero of the Western Front was Sergeant York, who captured several regiments of Germans by popping up in unexpected places and making noises like an armored division. When the Germans discovered York was only one man, and a noncom at that, they threw up their hands in disgust. Once their hands were up, it was an easy matter to take them prisoner.

Our boys were under the splendid leadership of Pershing, while the British were stimulated by Haig and Haig. The Germans put their faith in generals named von Hindenburg, von Moltke, and von Zeppelin, and boasted that the war was "as good as von." The German soldiers were often called Huns by the Americans, and the ones with bad dispositions were known as Sour Krauts.

CHAPTER XLI.

PEACE.

WORLD WAR I was ended by declaring an Armistice Day. Troops were urgently needed at home for parades.

President Wilson at once sailed for France to help redraw the map of Europe, which badly needed it because the colors had run. He traveled all over Europe and was triumphantly hailed at a number of points.[1] Streets, railroad stations, and children were named after him as quickly as they could be built or born.

Wilson brought home with him an engraved invitation to join the League of Nations, a fashionable club in Geneva, and thought everyone would be pleased. But Senator Lodge, who was not a joiner, thought there were enough good clubs right here in this country. Some say he turned his back on the future, which was discourteous, to say the least. At any rate America

[1] Fourteen, to be exact.

never joined, and the League couldn't get along without American support, which had been included in the budget.

The war left Europeans with huge debts, and they were at first discouraged about their ability to pay them. When they discovered that they only owed the money to the United States, their relief was considerable. This was called War Relief.

Redrawing the map of Europe.

CHAPTER XLII.

PROHIBITION.

ABOUT this time a group called the Drys, who wore tall hats and carried umbrellas, got into a terrific wrangle with a group of thirsty people called the Wets.

At first the Wets did not take the Drys seriously, and were mildly amused at their dry humor. They became alarmed, however, when the Drys commenced trying out on them what was called a Noble Experiment. This lasted for about thirteen years and led to the development of the following:

1. *Home brew*—a drink made in bathtubs that left a dark brown ring.[1]

[1] See Whisky Ring, above.

2. *Moonshine*—a brew made in caldrons under the light of a new moon while chanting incantations like:

> *Toil and worry,*
> *Tongue feels furry;*
> *Trouble, trouble,*
> *Seeing double.*
> *Newts and lizzards,*
> *Burns through gizzards;*
> *Awful, awful,*
> *Quite unlawful.*

3. *Bootleggers*—men who delivered liquor to Wild Parties in boots, after which it was divided up and drunk out of ladies' slippers.

4. *Speakeasies*—places where people spoke more easily after their tongues had been loosened.

Wild parties.

CHAPTER XLIII.

HARDING: A WEAK PRESIDENT.

HARDING became president as the result of mistaken identity. The Republican presidential convention was held in a smoke-filled room, and visibility was so poor that Harding was mistaken for Hoover.[1] Once he was nominated, the Republicans had no choice but to go through with it and elect him. They apologized to Hoover, however, and assured him that his turn would come soon.

Harding came from a small town in Ohio called Normalcy, which he was always wanting to return to.

DISARMAMENT CONFERENCE.

About the only good thing for which Harding is remembered is the Disarmament Conference. This was a meeting held in Washington at which each nation sought to disarm all the others. There was great enthusiasm, and the delegates all went home with souvenirs which they melted down and made into cannons.

TEAPOT DOME.

The government had a large, dome-shaped mountain full of oil that it was quietly saving for the Navy. Unfortunately, Harding shared this secret information with one of the boys in

Fall sneaked out the oil in teapots.

the back room, a poker player by the name of Fall. Then the trouble started. Fall sneaked out the oil in teapots and sold them to Big Businessmen, who got a few cents back for return-

[1] Both of them wore high stiff collars. In difficult times, these helped them keep their chins up.

ing the empties. As might be imagined, tea drinkers all over the country were indignant and demanded that Fall be sent to prison for causing a shortage of teapots. They also said that President Harding's hands were not clean, though he had always been considered a neat dresser back in Normalcy. All of this upset Harding and made it hard for him to digest crab meat, which led to Coolidge.[1]

———◆———

CHAPTER XLIV

COOLIDGE: A QUIET PRESIDENT.

COOLIDGE was sworn in by his father, who was a justice of the peace, at two o'clock in the morning. He wanted to lose no time drawing his pay as president. He swore to uphold the Constitution, which Harding had let sag a bit, and then went back to bed and slept soundly until time for his inauguration.

The most memorable thing about Coolidge was his dour silence. He is widely known for what he did not say. His favorite expressions were "Yes" and "No," and even these he used sparingly and often delegated to a subordinate.

A thrifty New Englander, Cal (as he was called to save a syllable) also saved string, paper clips, and picture calendars from the general store in Plymouth, Vermont.

Coolidge was reelected on the slogan, "Keep Cool With Coolidge." Since it had been an unusually hot summer, this campaign promise won widespread support, and Coolidge lived up to it through the fall and winter. Just before the next election he made one of his longest and most eloquent speeches. This speech is of such importance that its full text is printed here.

"I do not choose to run."

[1] Many believe that Harding was innocent and put the whole blame on Fall. This is the source of the expression "Fall guy."

———◆———

CHAPTER XLV.

THE ROARING TWENTIES.

THIS was a very noisy time. Business was booming, the stock market was crashing, and racketeers were making a racket. There was a great deal of roaring, especially by young persons in their twenties who, being members of the Lost Generation, were always bumping into things. Because of all this noise, people could not hear themselves think. It was therefore not an especially thoughtful period.

Among the popular pastimes of this era were such strenuous activities as channel swimming, flagpole sitting, goldfish swallowing, and trial marriage. A dance called the Charleston was engaged in by people known as "hot" dancers because they never took off their raccoon coats.

Gangsters, or Big Shots, who had scars on their faces to identify them, were driven around in long black limousines by Little Shots. Among the most famous gangsters were Al Capone, Little Caesar, and a sinister Oriental woman by the name of Ma Jong. Big Shots loved funerals, and were always shooting other Big Shots so they could send them horseshoe-shaped floral pieces inscribed "Good Luck."

One Big Shot and two Little Shots.

It was the heyday of sports. Famous sports included Babe
Ruth, Jack Dempsey, and Bobby Jones. In a spectacular boxing upset, Dempsey was knocked out by a college man named
Tunney, who had a volume of Shakespeare's plays tucked in
his glove and was thus able to give his opponent the works.

Important writers at this time included such persons as
H. L. Mencken, who was known as "The American Mercury,"
and Theodore Dreiser, who was known as "The American
Tragedy." Many of the leading writers, like F. Scott Fitzgerald
and Ernest Hemingway, lived in Paris to be near Gertrude
Stein and Alice Talkless, whom they could understand better
in French.

THE CRASH.

About this time stocks became exceedingly common. Everyone had a few thousand shares and turned at once to the
financial section of the newspaper to see how much richer he
was than yesterday. Stocks were usually bought on the margin,
especially by those who wanted to be closer to the gilt edge.

Financial experts, called Paper Prophets, were forecasting
that stocks would go higher. But suddenly, on a dark day known
as Black Tuesday, the stock market, which was a big building
on Wall Street,[1] collapsed. The accident is attributed to panic
among stock-exchange employees when someone shouted that
bears were loose in the place.

After this unfortunate occurrence everything was quieter and
the Roaring Twenties died to a whimper.

CHAPTER XLVI.

THE GREAT DEPRESSION.

THE FALL of the stock market caused a great depression right
in the middle of Wall Street. For most of his term, President

[1] Near the corner of Dun and Bradstreet.

Visibility was limited.

Hoover tried manfully to fill it up. He used ticker tape, raccoon coats, pocket flasks, unsold copies of books on Technocracy, and notes from foreign governments thanking him for declaring a moratorium, which permitted them to delay paying debts they did not intend to pay at all. The hole remained about as large as ever, though, and was a menace to traffic.

Hoover insisted that "prosperity was just around the corner," along with rainbows and cups of coffee and pieces of pie in the sky. But people distrusted him because they didn't believe he could see around the corner with so many apple sellers in the way. Visiblity was also limited by the grass that was growing in the streets.

THE BONUS ARMY.

The only war during Hoover's administration was with the Bonus Army. This was an ill-housed and ill-clothed band of veterans, so ill-fed that they were down to skin and bonus. They mistakenly marched on Washington in order to get some money from the government, not knowing that all the money was at Fort Knox. They camped for a while in the lobby of one of the large hotels, but finally left in tears, partly from disappointment and partly from tear gas.

CHAPTER XLVII

F.D.R.

F.D.R., or That Man, as he was known by Republicans, was born with a silver cigarette holder in his mouth. He was elected president despite the opposition of those who were in his class at Groton and Harvard, and thus became known as a Traitor to his Class. Except for his persistence in wearing an old school tie, he dressed very well.

As president, he surrounded himself with a group of intimates known as Fireside Chaps. These included men with such picturesque names as Harry the Hop, Tommy the Cork, The Old Curmudgeon, Moley,[1] and Ironpants Johnson, a chap who must have had trouble sitting down. Most of F.D.R.'s aides had been college professors all their lives, and insisted on wearing mortarboards instead of top hats. They formed a society known as the Brain Trust—so called because they trusted each other's brains —and let themselves into the White House by a back door that could be opened only with a Phi Beta Kappa key.

F.D.R.'s alphabetical agencies.

F.D.R. was elected president four times, largely because he was on a horse in the middle of the stream every November. A vote for F.D.R. was a vote for progress, and everyone wanted to see him get ahead, at least until he reached dry land.

Outstanding accomplishments of F.D.R. were the following:

[1] A character out of *The Wind in the Willows*.

1. Priming the pump. This led to a flow of milk, honey, 3.2 beer, and ultimately to the Repeal of Prohibition.

2. Packing the court. F.D.R. packed the Supreme Court in a large box and was about to ship it off when cries were heard inside. He had forgotten to leave air holes.

3. Establishing alphabetical agencies, chief of which were AAA (obviously the first), NRA (which set up game laws to protect the vanishing blue eagle), CCC (Spanish for "Yes, yes, yes"), and FDR.

4. Inventing such things as bonedoggling (a means of feeding a dog the same bone over and over), the New Deal (with the help of Ely Culbertson), the Roosevelt Dollar (which had the gold content taken out of it to keep it from turning yellow), etc.

5. Giving away overage destroyers, such as the Nine Old Men.

6. Recognizing Russia. Since Russia was a bear that walked like a man, this wasn't easy.

CHAPTER XLVIII.

WORLD WAR II.

WORLD WAR II began because the Germans felt they needed a *Lebensraum*, or living room. They already had a kitchen, bedroom, and bath, but they wanted a place where they could entertain guests. The Germans at that time were under the leadership of a Furor named Heil Hitler, who looked like Charlie Chaplin but was only in the newsreels.

Hitler, who never tired of walking, marched into Poland with his panthers. He also marched into the Low Countries. This was easier because it was downhill all the way. When people resisted, despite their having signed a treaty of friendship, Hitler blew them to blitz and destroyed their favorite dives with his dive bombers.

A furor.

THE AXES.

The Germans thought themselves supermen, that is to say *Deutschlandersuberalles*, and drove all who were not 100 percent into grottoes. Everyone had to be full of Nordic blood, grade A and pasteurized, and had to have a blond grandmother. The only exceptions were the Italians and Japanese, who made the team because of what they did to the Ethiopians and the Chinese. The leader of the Italians was an unwell person called Ill Duce, who made the trains run on time because he had a horror of being late to meet Hitler.

Russia was one of the Axes for a while, and helped chop up Poland and Finland,[1] but there was a change of plans.

AMERICA ENTERS THE WAR.

At first England did most of the fighting, despite the fact that it was overrun by exiled kings related to the Royal Family and seeking refuge in the House of Windsor.

The United States did not enter the war until the Japanese

[1] The Russians were afraid of Finland, a large and powerful nation that constantly threatened their security with warlike acts such as playing the music of Sibelius.

attacked Pearl Harbor, whereupon our forces landed in North Africa to confuse the Japs. Among the important contributions made by the United States to the war effort were:

1. Lend-Lease, which was a delicate way of giving things to our proud Allies.

2. American No, How? We were always asking our Allies if they knew how to do something or other. When they said, "No, How?" we told them.

3. Ingenious instruments of war. These included hedge-clippers used to trim the hedgerows in France; pogo sticks for island hopping in the Pacific; atom bombs, used to tidy up Japan; and floating harbors, which turned the tide.

———◆———

CHAPTER XLIX.

TRUMAN: A LIVELY PRESIDENT.

NEAR THE END of World War II, Harry S. Truman stepped into F.D.R.'s shoes. Since he had once been a haberdasher, he knew the shoes didn't fit, and said so. One of the first things he did was to start what he called the Fair Deal. This was an understatement, since he obviously thought it better than fair and really rather good.

Truman was an accomplished pianist, but there is a difference

An accomplished pianist.

of opinion as to what else he accomplished. "They laughed when I sat down to play," he said, referring to the time a Republican removed the piano stool. His repertoire included "The Missouri Waltz," which he always played when he was asked for an encore, and he was always asked.[1]

Probably no president has had such a colorful vocabulary as Truman. When a Washington music critic used some harsh words about his daughter Margaret's singing, President Truman used some words that were even harsher and were widely quoted, sometimes with dashes or only initials.

Truman's election to a second term was an upset. It particularly upset the Republicans and the poll takers. Some think his opponent, Thomas E. Dewey, was defeated because he was compared to the little man on a wedding cake. This cost him the votes of hundreds of thousands of men who were unhappily married.

THE COMMUNISTS.

A great deal of trouble was caused at this time and later by the Communists. During what was called the Century of the Common Man,[2] they claimed to be the commonest of all. The Communists lived in underground cells, but came out once a year, on May 1st, to see whether they cast a shadow. They always did.

The Communists owe their origin to Karl, the funniest of the Marx Brothers, who described what was going to happen to the rest of the world in a book called *Das Kaput-all*. It is widely discussed, especially by those who have never read it. Communists go around with clenched fists and thus are terribly hard to shake hands with.

---

[1] There was sure to be someone around who wanted to become an ambassador.

[2] A phrase thought up by Henry Wallace while experimenting with hybrid corn, which may explain why it is a little corny.

Hard to shake hands with.

HISS AND MCCARTHY.

The name of Alger Hiss threw a scare into the country. It was on everyone's tongue, which made a meeting of more than two people sound like a snake convention. What frightened people about Hiss was that he had something to do with some papers hidden in a pumpkin, and it was not even Halloween.[1]

Even more terrifying was Senator Joseph R. McCarthy, who thought there was a Communist under every bed, and often awoke people in the middle of the night with his poking around. During the day McCarthy looked for Communists in the State Department—under desks.[2] A "Joe Should Go" movement was started, and though its backers did not say where they thought Joe should go, everyone had a pretty good idea. Finally McCarthy was censored for something "unbecoming a Senator." No doubt it was his rumpled suit.

[1] It was perhaps with Halloween in mind that some called it a witch hunt.
[2] First he said he had found 205. Later he reduced the number to 57, and still later to one—whose name slipped his mind. Whether it was the name or his mind that was slippery is controversial, and therefore cannot be discussed.

The Korean War was at first referred to as a Police Action, but after a while we ran out of police and had to send soldiers.

General MacArthur wanted to bomb the Chinese bases, but since all Chinese look alike, President Truman was afraid he might also hit an occasional baritone or tenor. So he decided to call MacArthur home for a ticker tape parade. "I have five stars and six Oak Leaf Clusters," said General MacArthur. "How many have you?" But Truman managed to convince him that a Commander-in-Chief outranks a Supreme Commander. General MacArthur then left the military service and became Chairman of the Board, a rank in which there is no such thing as over-age in grade. Upon undertaking his new career, he said with customary vigor, "Old soldiers never die, they just fade. Away!"

———◆———

CHAPTER L.

EISENHOWER: A LIKABLE PRESIDENT.

GENERAL EISENHOWER WAS elected president because he was a Father Image.[1] He was also a National Hero. This was something the country needed—to go with its National Parks, National Monuments, and National Cemetery. His opponent, Governor Adlai E. Stevenson, had a broader forehead,[2] but Eisenhower had a broader grin. Also the slogan "I Like Ike" was better for chanting at rallies than "I Adore Adlai." An old Army man, Eisenhower promised to clean up "the mess in Washington," probably by bringing in some experienced mess sergeants. He also said he would "go to Korea," which everyone thought was a Good Idea, except those who had been there.

Key positions in President Eisenhower's cabinet were filled

[1] See the story of Father Image, Mother Image, and the three little Images.
[2] An egghead forehead, which stops at nothing.

with men like Secretary of Defense Charles E. Wilson, formerly head of General Motors, who said that "Whatever is good for General Motors is good for General Electric," [1] and Secretary of the Treasury George M. Humphrey, a Cleveland industrial magnet, who pulled in the money. His Secretary of State was John Foster Dulles, who spent most of his time on airplanes and invented Brinkmanship, the most popular game since Monopoly.

After four years of Eisenhower, Prosperity ran for a second term—no, after four years of Prosperity, Eisenhower ran for a second term. Once again the Democrats ran Adlai Stevenson,

Ran for a second term.

who had some jokes left over from the first campaign.[2] But Eisenhower won, having impressed voters with his ability to stand in a moving car without holding on to anything. He proved it by raising both hands over his head.

During his second term, the National Debt rose a few billion, but Ike's golf score came down several strokes. He traveled widely—to England, France, India, Augusta, and Palm Springs. Everywhere he was surrounded by admiring crowds, which sometimes pressed in so close that he was unable to swing.

[1] And, presumably, General Telephone and General Eisenhower.
[2] As well as a hole in his shoe from all that running for office.

UN stands for the United Nations. It also stands for a great many other things, since it is remarkably patient. It is made up of slightly deaf delegates who wear earphones and always have the name of their country on a sign in front of them so they can remember where they are from.

The UN is dominated by the Great Powers, which are the United States, England, France, and Russia. The Great Powers are in turn dominated by the Veto Powers, which are mostly Russia. At times there is more power than light.

Nor should we neglect the Underdeveloped Nations and Emerging People of Africa and Asia, which have been underdeveloped and unemerged long enough.

The chief purpose of the UN is to keep the peace, if anyone can find it.

SPUTNIK.

The Russians, who were thought behind in science, suddenly proved they were ahead by firing a rocket, called sputnik, which went into Orbit. At night it could be seen with (pardon the expression) the naked eye. In the ensuing Race for Space,[1] Russia got a head start with its sputniks, but the United States was second to none when it came to beatniks. Oddly, Russia has always been famous for beards. Yet, while a bearded beatnik is commonplace, a bearded sputnik is virtually unknown. Russia put up bigger rockets, but with our Vanguards, Titans, Atlases, Thors, Nikes, Mercuries, Redstones, Minute Men, and Polarises, we proved our superiority at thinking up names.

The Russian sputniks led also to a race to see which country could produce more engineers. The United States, which had been a democracy, seemed to be slipping into a rule by scientists, known as the Slide Rule.

[1] See also the Arms Race and the Rat Race. No wonder there is a Race Problem.

———◆———

CHAPTER LI.

KENNEDY: A YOUTHFUL PRESIDENT.

AFTER EIGHT YEARS OF EISENHOWER, many Americans wanted a change, for instance a president with hair. The choice was between two men well qualified in this regard, Vice President Richard Nixon, who had come up from poverty, and Senator John F. Kennedy, who was born rich and stayed that way. When young Nixon graduated from high school, his family chipped in and bought him a watch. When young Kennedy graduated from high school, his father gave him a million dollars, because he already had a watch.

Nixon and Kennedy carried on their campaign through a series of Great Debates on television. Nixon was expected to win because he had been a great debater in college. Besides, he had been on a television program once before, with his dog, and had had everyone in tears. Unfortunately, however, in preparation for his first debate with Kennedy he had his face made up [1] by a retired mortician. Voters were afraid Mr. Nixon wouldn't last through the four-year term, or even the TV program.

Kennedy won the election, though by a very small margin of popular votes.[2] He was the youngest president ever elected.

[1] His mind was already made up.
[2] No one thought to tally the unpopular votes.

Those who thought his voice might change after he had been in office a while did not realize that the New England accent has been with us for more than three hundred years.

Kennedy tried to arouse public interest in his program by calling it the New Frontier, stealing the idea from the sign on a saloon in a TV Western. But people were chiefly interested in Mrs. Kennedy, who looked the way most women wished they looked and the way some of them thought they, too, would

The New Frontier.

look if they bought their gowns in Paris.[1] For the first time in many years, the White House echoed with the voices of small children, and when the lights went on in the wee hours of the morning it was not because of an international crisis.

Whereas Eisenhower had surrounded himself with Army officers and industrialists, Kennedy chose for his aides mostly

1. Members of his family (Kennedys, Fitzgeralds, and Nepotists).
2. Harvard men (there was a mass migration from Cambridge, Mass.).
3. Athletes (not likely to become winded when making long speeches).
4. Movie stars ("We must act," Kennedy kept saying).

[1] Everybody referred to her as Jackie, as if they knew her personally and belonged to the same riding club.

The only suggestion of the Army was in the person of a non-com, Sergeant Shriver, who headed what was called the Peace Corpse, peace having become a dead issue.

Kennedy had trouble with Cuba and Fiddle Castro, a man with several strings to his bow. As one historian says, "Kennedy's intelligence was at fault.[1] He apparently didn't know that the bay where an invasion took place was full of pigs. The pigs got in the way of landing craft and their squealing so unnerved the invaders that they went all to pieces and were easily defeated.

Things went better for Kennedy when he had an eyeball-to-eyeball confrontation with Castro's friend Krush-shove, who blinked first. It was Kennedy's finest hour.[2]

CHAPTER LII.

JOHNSON: A TEXAS PRESIDENT.

LYNDON BAINES JOHNSON was called LBJ.[3] His wife was a lady bird, which was not unusual in Texas.

Johnson founded the Great Society, members of which were known as "y'all." Instead of dues, they paid taxes.[4] LBJ showed them his scar and even his popularity poll. He also showed them how to pick up a dog by the ears.

One of his memorable achievements was turning out the lights in the White House so that nobody could see what was going on.

---

[1] Some think it was not Kennedy's intelligence but that of his advisers that should be blamed.

[2] It may even have been an hour and a half. Anyhow, it was a record.

[3] Among other things.

[4] When Johnson said "taxes" it sounded like "Texas," and vice versa.

Showed them his scar.

VIETNAM.

Somehow, under Eisenhower and Kennedy the United States had become involved in a war in Vietnam. How we got into the war no one seemed to know. There was, of course, the domino theory that the war was promoted by Big Business, especially the makers of dominoes. Others thought it was to provide a place where Bob Hope could visit our troops.

Johnson made improvements in the war by sending in airplanes, tanks, and escalators.[1] He also made it possible to keep score by publishing the body count each week. Despite this, many people called it an Immoral War,[2] especially idealistic young men of draft age. "Hell no. We won't go!" they chanted when asked to leave the Dean's office. They were good humored about it, however, often shouting "Ho-ho, ho-ho Chi Minh!"

What kept the war going was that somebody was always seeing a light at the end of a tunnel. What could it be? Someone with a lantern? A swarm of fireflies? You couldn't tell until you got a closer look.

Peace negotiators in Paris made motions [3] and then, having agreed on the shape of the table, tabled them.

Johnson decided not to run for another term, hoping this would bring peace in Vietnam or at any rate make everyone happy. He returned to his ranch in Texas, which some felt he had never left, and settled down among the cowpokes, slowpokes, and pigs in pokes.

GAPS.

It was during Johnson's administration that certain gaps developed. These included the Generation Gap, the Communication Gap, the Credibility Gap, and the Gap Gap, this last being the gap between gaps, which was never long.[4]

---

[1] These last were to prove to his critics that everything was on the up and up.

[2] Unlike the usual Moral War.

[3] Some of them threatening.

[4] What was long, however, was the hair on young people, which came down to their shoulders and sometimes to their hippies.

CHAPTER LIII.

NIXON: A PERSISTENT PRESIDENT.

WHEN Eisenhower was president, Richard Nixon was within a heartbeat of the presidency, and went around carrying a stethoscope. Then, when he ran against Kennedy and lost by a Narrow Margin, everyone thought he was through. When he wasn't elected governor of California, even he began to have doubts. How much lower could he go? Should he run for Mayor of Whittier? Reaching the depths, he went into a law firm.

Close Race.

But Nixon, known by some as Tricky Dick, came back.[1] In a Close Race, he defeated Hubert Humphrey. Voters chose him over Humphrey because:

1. Humphrey was in the shadow of Johnson and hard to see.

[1] Was it really Nixon or someone with a similar nose known as the New Nixon?

2. He had a loose tongue, and it might fall out.

3. Everyone worried about having a president who would be called HHH.

Nixon became interested in Welfare. Improving the lot of the president, he had a lot in Florida and a lot in California, each with a house on it. He also became interested in pollution. "Let me make this perfectly clear," he said, gazing at Lake Michigan.

It was under Nixon[1] that America sent a man to the moon to get some rocks. There were those who objected to such an expensive trip, thinking we had enough rocks already.

On some issues Nixon was inclined to stand pat.[2] On others he weakened, as with the uniforms for the White House guards, which he gave up when the opera company asked for them back.

Uniforms for White House guards.

Nixon's vice president, Spiro Agnew, became a Household Word.[3]

[1] Actually it was over him.
[2] "I can stand Pat," he said, when someone asked him about his wife.
[3] See also Drano and Fab.

CHAPTER LIV.

CONCLUSION.

THE UNITED STATES IS now entering a New Era.[1] Its path is fraught with peril, full of hazards, and strewn with obstacles. What this country needs is a good street sweeper.

[1] What, again?

THE END

FINAL EXAMINATION.

1. Contemplate the consequences if World War II had been waged before World War I.

2. Write a short factual or imaginative composition on one of the following subjects:

    (*a*) Why I Was Not Old Enough to Vote for McKinley.

    (*b*) A Descent into the Depths of the Depression.

    (*c*) Should Prohibition Have Been Prohibited? Or, Denatured vs. Good-natured Alcohol.

    (*d*) Incidents in the life of Roosevelt. (Before you conclude, explain in detail which Roosevelt you have been writing about.)

3. Quote at length.

4. Aren't you glad it's the government that owes the national debt and not you?

5. Make a list of the modern conveniences in your home that you would not have had to repair in 1865.

6. Lock all the doors and try to corner a market.

7. Discuss in detail whatever you still do not know about American history.

8. How can you become a better citizen? What's stopping you?

GLOSSARY OF TERMS.

America: Same as United States of America, much to the annoyance of persons living in Canada and the Latin American countries.

Ambassador: Person with enough influence to be appointed and enough wealth to be able to serve.

Boom: Opposite of Bust.

Bust: Opposite of Boom, except when applied to women.

Communist: 1. A Communist. 2. (*Americanism, unfortunately not yet obsolete*) Anyone who disagrees with you.

Conservative: A man who saves his money (even before women and children).

Damnyankee: Southernism for Vermonter.

Democrat: Opposite of Republican.

Frontier: Area occupied by persons always in the van, along with their furniture.

Inauguration: Ceremony during which the President stands in the rain with his hat off.

Liberal: Something everyone claims to be.

Peace: Short period of preparation for the next war.

Platform: Structure intended to give a lift to party morale.

Puritan: Person opposed to sin, especially in others.

Republican: Opposite of Democrat.

Radical: Opposite of almost anything.

Red: See Russia.

Russia: See red.

Satellite: Neighboring country attracted into Russian orbit by removal of trade barriers, food supplies, and leading citizens.

Suffrage: Pain caused women by unaccustomed exercise of their franchise.

Two-party System: Political system composed of two parties, the Ins and the Outs.

Richard Armour may be playful and irreverent in his treatment of history, but he began as a respectable scholar. A Phi Beta Kappa graduate of Pomona College and a Ph.D. from Harvard, he has held fellowships in England and France, and his first books, which he says he wrote "to get promoted," were meticulously researched biographies. He has taught at a number of colleges and universities, was a Dean of the Faculty, and has lectured at universities in Europe and Asia as an American Specialist for the State Department. He is currently a lecturer and guest-in-residence on many campuses.

A contributor of light verse and prose humor and satire to over two hundred magazines in the United States and England, he has written more than forty books in a wide variety of fields. *It All Started with Columbus* was his first best seller and led to a series of six *It All Started with* books. Also, as he says, "It did the greatest thing for me that a book can do for a teacher. It eventually enabled me to stop teaching." In addition to the spoofs and parodies for which he has become well known, he has written a number of books for children. One of these, *On Your Marks: A Package of Punctuation*, with a foreword by Ogden Nash, has been made into an animated film and is widely used in schools.

Richard Armour has told of his own life (mixing fact and fiction) in such books as *Drug Store Days, Golf Is a Four-Letter Word, Through Darkest Adolescence,* and *My Life with Women.* He is married, has a son and daughter, and lives in Claremont, California.

ABOUT THE ILLUSTRATOR

Campbell Grant, who has illustrated eleven of Richard Armour's books, was with Walt Disney for twelve years as a character creator and story man. During World War II he worked with Frank Capra on documentaries. Since 1960 he has been actively interested in archaeology and has written three books on the subject—*The Rock Paintings of the Chumash, Rock Art of the American Indian,* and *Rock Drawings of the Coso Range.* The first of these was picked as one of the top 25 books of the year for outstanding design at the 1966 American Association of University Presses book show. His fourth book on prehistoric art will feature the cliff dweller and Navajo paintings in the Canyon de Chelly, Arizona. He teaches art, travels widely, and is active in conservation matters. Living idyllically on a ranch near Santa Barbara, he raises avocados and has a talented writer-wife and four children.

Catalog

If you are interested in a list of fine Paperback
books, covering a wide range of subjects
and interests, send your name and address,
requesting your free catalog, to:

McGraw-Hill Paperbacks
1221 Avenue of Americas
New York, N.Y. 10020